The Safe Baby

Also by Debra Smiley Holtzman

THE PANIC-PROOF PARENT: CREATING A
SAFE LIFESTYLE FOR YOUR FAMILY

The Safe Baby

A Do-It-Yourself Guide to Home Safety

DEBRA SMILEY HOLTZMAN

SENTIENT PUBLICATIONS

First Sentient Publications edition 2005
Copyright © 2005 by Debra Smiley Holtzman

In a time of rapid change, it is difficult to ensure that all of the information contained in this book is entirely up to date. Therefore, the author and publisher accept no responsibility for any errors or omissions and specifically disclaim any liability, loss, or risk that is incurred as a consequence, directly or indirectly, of the use and/or application of any of the contents of this book. Readers are encouraged to confirm the information contained herein with other sources. The ultimate responsibility for child safety resides with you, the caregiver. The mention of specific products or services in this book does not constitute or imply a recommendation or endorsement by the author, unless it is explicitly stated.

The first aid procedures described in this book are designed to assist you in the event of an emergency until medical treatment can be obtained. They are for reference purposes. The author advises all readers to complete a certified first aid course and CPR course. This book is not intended as a substitute for proper first aid training. In the event of a medical emergency, readers are advised to promptly consult with a physician or other health professional.

A paperback original

Printed in the United States of America

Cover design by Kim Johansen, Black Dog Design
Book design by Nicholas Cummings

Library of Congress Cataloging-in-Publication Data

Holtzman, Debra Smiley.
   The safe baby : a do-it yourself guide to home safety / by Debra Smiley Holtzman.-- 1st Sentient Publications ed.
      p. cm.
   Includes bibliographical references and index.
   ISBN 1-59181-029-9
   1. Home accidents--Prevention. I. Title.
TX150.H652 2004
643'.0289--dc22
                                                                2004012133

Printed in the United States of America

10 9 8 7 6 5 4 3 2

SENTIENT PUBLICATIONS

A Limited Liability Company
1113 Spruce Street
Boulder, CO 80302
www.sentientpublications.com

Acknowledgments

I especially thank my editor, Drollene P. Brown; my agent, Pamela Harty, of The Knight Agency; Connie Shaw and the staff at Sentient Publications; my husband, Robert Holtzman, M.D.; my mother, Harriet Smiley; and my sisters, Madeleine Levy and Karen Pollack.

Thanks to the many organizations and governmental agencies and the people who spoke for them who promptly and graciously answered my inquires, supplied me with information, or reviewed sections of the book: National SAFE KIDS campaign, especially Angela D. Mickalide, Ph.D.,CHES, Marisa Peacock, and Jennifer Medearis Costello; Centers for Disease Control and Prevention, especially Dr. Joseph Piesman; Environmental Protection Agency, especially Linda Rutsch; Food and Drug Administration; National Highway Traffic Safety Administration; USDA Meat and Poultry Hotline; Environmental Working Group; Florida Department of Health; American Academy of Pediatrics; La Leche League International; First Candle/SIDS Alliance, especially Laura Reno and Heather Boyer; National Center on Shaken Baby Syndrome, especially Amy Wicks; Alliance for Healthy Homes, especially Don Ryan; National Association of State Public Interest Research Groups (PIRGs); Consumer Federation of American, especially Rachael Weintraub; American Lyme Disease Foundation, especially David L. Weld; Burn Prevention Council, especially JoAnne McLauglin; Beyond Pesticides, especially Jay Feldman.

Thanks also to The Danny Foundation, especially Jack Walsh; NSF International, especially Dave Purkiss and Thomas J. Bruursema; SafetyBeltSafe U.S. A., especially Stephanie Tombrello and Cheryl Kim; Food Allergy and Anaphylaxis, especially Eileen Sexton; Safe Tables our Priority, especially Susan Vaughn Grooters; National Program for Playground Safety, especially Donna Thompson, Ph.D.; National Fire Protection Administration; Florida Department of Community Affairs, Division of Emergency Management; American Red Cross, especially Rocky Lopes, Ph.D.; Healthy Building Network, especially Bill Walsh; and the National

Resource Center for Health and Safety in Child Care, especially Barbara U. Hamilton.

For reviewing sections of the book and providing information, thanks to Robert M. Carter of PrepareFirst, Inc.; Monte Levy; Dana Best, MD, MPH; and Dr. Neil Pollack of Brookhaven Country Day Camp.

A special thanks to my colleagues in Florida for answering all my questions, reviewing sections of the book, and supplying information: Sue Englund, RN, Memorial Regional Hospital; Jerry Goodman, Safe Pest Eliminator; Cecilia Haroon; Mark Horowitz, bicycle transportation consultant; JoAnn Chambers-Emerson, RN, Florida Poison Information Center, Tampa General Hospital; Howard Rosen, RS, Pamela Santucci and Tom Mueller of Broward County Health Department; Paul Goldberg, MD; and Christina Stevens, DVM.

Thank you, Adam and Laura. You are my inspiration.

This book is dedicated to
my husband, Robert
my children, Adam and Laura
my parents, Irving and Harriet Smiley
and my father-in-law, Julian Holtzman

Contents

Introduction

As a parent or grandparent, your greatest concern is the safety of the precious children in your care. If you are also handy with tools and tend to do projects around the house yourself rather than hire someone, you may need guidelines on occasion to make your home safer for the entire family. This book will tell you how to do certain projects yourself and also inform you of the situations in which it is crucial that you hire a professional.

One thing I always tell parents in my safety classes is this: You don't have to take the advice of well-meaning friends and relatives. Uncle Frank may see nothing wrong with smoking cigarettes in your home, and Aunt Polly may insist that you use her antique crib for your baby. Stand your ground! You will learn a lot about safety as you read this book; stick to the best safety and health practices for your baby.

Having told you to follow my advice, I'd like you to know that you can cut yourself some slack. The last thing I want is for parents to be overwhelmed with all these dos and don'ts. You'll get lots of facts here to help you keep your child safe, but the greatest safety is found in your love. With your love will come the vigilance that I write so much about; you can watch without making yourself and your child nervous wrecks. Remember this: you don't have to do everything perfectly to usher your child into adulthood. Have fun with your baby! These are precious years.

If you have questions not covered in this book, I invite you to email your question or concern to safebook@aol.com. Who knows? Perhaps your question—or your solution—will be featured in my next child-safety book.

Part I

Room to Room for Safety

In Part I we'll consider three specific rooms in the home, the ones in which your little darling may well spend the most time at first: nursery (Chapter 1), kitchen (Chapters 2 and 3), and bathroom (Chapter 4). It will be obvious to you that some of the same guidelines are to be followed in other rooms, as well. But I don't have to tell you that—after all, you're a do-it-yourselfer. Remember previous tips when you walk into the living room or out in the yard.

Creating a Safe Nursery

The nursery is where the new baby will spend most of his time. I'm sure you'll want to decorate the room beautifully, giving it lots of little touches that will make it a pleasant place. While you are doing this, you'll want to make safety your first priority. Safety is your top concern when it comes to your baby and your home. That's why we're starting by making the nursery safe. (In addition to this chapter, there is information about keeping the nursery safe from chemicals in Chapter 11, "Environmental Hazards.")

How to Choose and Use Nursery Equipment

In the United States, about 20 babies suffocate or strangle each year after becoming trapped in a crib that is unsafe. That's why you should never compromise safety for savings when buying or acquiring a crib for your precious baby.

Choose the Right Crib

If possible, purchase a new crib. A secondhand crib may have missing or broken parts and—if the crib was built before 1991—an unsafe design. In addition, a used crib is not likely to have the manufacturer's instructions, and worse, it may have been recalled.

As you shop for your baby's new crib, make sure the product meets Consumer Product Safety Commission (CPSC) standards. (See Appendix E, "Helpful Resources," for contact information for CPSC.) In addition, look for the Juvenile Products Manufacturers Association (JPMA) certification label. If you find that you must buy or accept a secondhand crib, be sure to test it according to the seven guidelines in the sidebar.

If the secondhand crib you have does not meet those checklist guidelines, it should be destroyed, or at least completely modified, so that no one will consider putting a baby in it. (Creative folk may turn the rails into a flower bed . . . just don't let your toddler get into it!) You can also take the wood and metal from the crib to recycling centers. The mattress and plastic parts, however, must be consigned to a waste disposal center.

Use the Crib Safely

After a crib has passed your scrutiny-based, of course, on the safety standards we've discussed—there are a few more points to cover about using the crib safely. Note that some of the rules change as the child grows.

- The primary rule in using the crib safely is this: Put your healthy baby on his back to sleep. See the section (page 15) on sudden infant death syndrome (SIDS) to learn more about putting your baby safely to sleep.

DO IT YOURSELF!

Make a secondhand crib meet the safety test.

- The crib should be sturdy, with no missing hardware, or loose or rickety parts.
- Slats should be no more than 2 3/8 inches apart. If you are able to pass a soda can between the slats, they are too far apart. The baby's head could get caught.
- Post extensions at the corners of the crib should be less than 1/16 of an inch. Larger extensions can cause entanglement. A canopy bed can have larger extensions if they are at least 16 inches high.
- There should be no cutouts in the head- or footboard. Again, the baby's head could get stuck.
- Mattresses must fit snugly into the crib. You must not be able to put 2 adult fingers between the mattress and crib sides. Baby can suffocate if his head or body becomes wedged between the mattress and the crib sides.
- The mattress support should be sturdy and not pull apart easily from the corner posts.
- The crib should be smooth. There should be no cracked or peeling paint, and no splinters or rough edges.

- A plastic mattress cover is okay, but never use a trash bag or plastic dry cleaning bag to do the job. The plastic film can cause suffocation.

- Use crib sheets that fit securely on all corners and sides. Check carefully for shrinkage after each wash. A child can pull poorly fitted sheets loose and become entrapped.

- When the child is in the crib, always have the side rail locked in its raised position.

- To prevent suffocation and reduce the likelihood of SIDS, remove from the baby's sleep area all soft, loose, and fluffy bedding such as pillows, blankets, quilts, bumper pads, stuffed toys, and other soft items in the crib. (See information about bumper pads in the next section.)

- Position any mobile or hanging crib toy out of your child's reach. This means that any such toy or crib gym must be removed when the baby begins to push up on her hands and knees, or when the baby is 5 months old, whichever comes first. These toys can strangle a baby. The baby can also pull pieces off the mobile, presenting a choking hazard.

- Don't hang anything on or above the crib with a ribbon or string longer than 7 inches.

- As soon as your baby can stand up, adjust the mattress to the lowest position.

- When your child first climbs out of the crib or when he is 35 inches tall, that is the time for a "big-kid" bed.

As long as your baby sleeps in the crib—regardless of whether it is new or used—periodically inspect it for missing hardware, chipped or peeled paint, holes and tears, loose threads, and strings.

Bumper Pads

Because of the concerns about SIDS and unintentional suffocation on soft bedding products, the use of soft bumper pads is not recommended by First Candle/SIDS Alliance. If you are concerned that if you do not use bumper pads, your baby, in rolling into the side of the crib, will sustain a bruise or injury to the head, you should understand that this is an unlikely occurrence. While it is true that a child's arms or legs can get stuck in the slats, serious injury is improbable. Moreover, a child can get an arm or leg stuck under or above a bumper pad.

If you *do* choose to use a bumper pad in your child's crib, select one that is not pillowlike. The pad should fit around the entire crib and have straps or ties at least in each corner, in the middle of each long side, and on both the top and the bottom edges. Trim off the straps after tying, to prevent strangulation. Once your baby begins to move around in the crib, the bumpers should be removed so she cannot get her face next to them. Bumpers can also be used by your baby to launch herself out of the crib once she can pull up and stand. Look for the new "breathable" mesh bumpers on the market today as a safer alternative to traditional bumpers in your baby's crib. Mesh bumpers also provide better visibility for seeing your sleeping baby.

Use Crib Rules as You Select Other Nursery Furniture

Choose all the furniture in your baby's room with care and use the rules you've learned about the crib to help you select other pieces. Be as wary in accepting other used furniture for the nursery as you are in accepting a crib. Make sure the furniture is sturdy, with no loose parts, no loose paint, and no rough, sharp edges. Take away any ties or loops. When buying furniture, make sure it meets current national safety standards. Look for the JPMA label and check with the CPSC to make sure it hasn't been recalled. You'll learn more about recalled products in Chapter 5, "Preventing Falls in the Home." We'll talk about ways to make ordinary furniture safer when we move to other rooms in the house.

> ### DO IT YOURSELF!
>
> **Make a safe zone around the crib.**
>
> To help reduce the risk of falls, strangulation, suffocation, and burns, create a safety zone around all furniture, especially the crib, playpen, changing table, and chairs.
>
> Do not position the furniture near windows, draperies, electrical cords, hanging wall decorations, heating sources, curtain cords, or climbable furniture.

Invest in a Baby Monitor

Now that your baby has a safe crib and safe furniture, can you be sure he is completely safe when you leave him alone in the room? You can't stay in the nursery all the time, but you need to know if your baby is in distress. Invest in a baby monitor and keep it on any time the child is alone in the room. If you get a portable unit, you can carry your part of it with you when you go from room to room. There are also video monitors that allow you to see, as well as hear, the baby. However, even if you have the newest, best monitor money can buy, nothing takes the place of checking on your child in person, to make sure everything is okay. Peek in once in a while to give yourself a smile.

Consider Carefully Your Choice of a Diaper Pail

One piece of essential equipment that may seem incidental is the diaper pail. When you get one, make sure it has a locking lid. A child can drown in the accumulated liquid in the pail. Do not use deodorizer tablets because once your child is getting around on his own, he may try to eat them, and they are poisonous. (Remember to wash your hands after each diaper change.)

Avoiding Common Hazards

Prevent Shocks and Burns

When an electrical outlet is not in use, cover it! Take care when you choose the outlet plugs. Your little explorer may find a way to pull one out . . . and when the plug comes out, it will go directly into his mouth. Then he is in danger of choking, as well as getting a bad burn. The lesson: Be sure the outlet protectors cannot be easily removed by children and are large enough so that children cannot choke on them. It is better to get safety covers that screw over the switch plate. Another way to make unused outlets safe is to place heavy furniture in front of them.

Prevent Strangulation

Think about every item in your home that has a ribbon or string attached to it. Make sure none of those items is near the crib. Don't tie pacifiers, necklaces, toys, or other items around a child's neck. In fact, don't attach anything with ribbon or string to a child's clothing. When you put the child into his crib, remove a bib or any other clothing that ties around his neck.

Take this admonition a bit further, outside the crib. Drawstrings from the hoods and necks of your child's jackets and sweatshirts (found in garments made before 1995) can be lethal. They can catch, not only on a crib, but also on playground equipment. Totally remove any drawstrings from the hood and neck of garments.

Follow these CPSC recommendations for children's clothing: Waist and bottom drawstrings should measure no more than 3 inches from where strings extend out of the garment. When your child leaves the nursery to go out to the playground, he should not only avoid garments with drawstrings, but he also should not wear over-sized clothing, necklaces, or scarves that could get snagged on playground equipment.

Now let's look at the curtains you put in the nursery. While you may have focused on the color when you dressed the window, there are a few other items to consider once the baby has come to reside in the room.

Studies have shown that most strangulation deaths from window cords happen when children are in places their parents think are safe: in a crib or child's bedroom. Where did you place the crib? An infant in a crib near a window can get tangled in a looped window cord while playing—or sleeping. A toddler wants to look

DO IT YOURSELF!

Avoid window cord strangulation.

- Don't allow your child to play with drapery or window blind cords.

- Don't put the child's crib or bed near a window. Keep all window-covering cords and chains out of reach of your child.

- Don't keep any furniture—toy box, chair, table, bench, or bookcase—near a window, drapery, or blind cord.

- Cut the loops on 2-corded horizontal blinds and attach separate tassels to prevent entanglement and strangulation.

- Install a permanent tie-down or tension device to vertical blinds, continuous loop systems, and drapery cords that need looped cords to function.*

- If you purchased blinds before 2001, install cord stops on the outer pull cord to keep your child from pulling down the inner cord.*

- When buying new window coverings, tell the salesman you want a short cord and ask for safety features to prevent child strangulation. Adjust the cords to their shortest possible length when installing. Better yet, look into cordless window coverings.

*Free window safety kits with safety tassels, tie-down devices, and cord stops are available from the Window Covering Safety Council. Go to www.windowcoverings.org or call the WCSC at (800) 506-4636. The website has diagrams and step-by-step instructions (under "How to Repair").

out the window, so no matter where his bed may be, he's likely to climb up onto furniture to get there. There is a danger that he will get caught in a window cord, then fall or jump.

The baby monitor won't help here unless it is a video monitor and you happen to be watching it at the time. These deaths are silent. The child won't be able to cry out for help.

See the sidebar for steps you can take to safeguard your child. The bottom line is this: Make sure every window treatment in your home is child-safe by repairing or replacing window coverings purchased before 2001 and by keeping all window-covering cords and chains out of reach of children. (For information about preventing falls from windows, see Chapter 5, "Preventing Falls in the Home.")

Prevent Choking

You may have noticed that infants and toddlers will put anything into their mouths—balloons, small toys . . . small anything! Even food cut into rounds or small pieces can choke a child, as you will see in Chapter 3, "More about the Kitchen: Keeping Your Baby's Food Safe." Putting things in their mouths is one way children explore their world. Choking is a leading cause of unintentional death of children. Children under age 3 are at the greatest risk.

There's another object you may not think comes under the heading of choking hazard: the baby bottle. Never prop it up so your baby can "feed herself." Holding your baby during bottle-feeding not only affords good bonding, but also reduces the risk of choking, tooth decay, and ear infections.

Another common object that should be inspected is the pacifier. The guard (shield) should be large and firm enough so that it will not fit into the child's mouth, and it should have ventilation holes in case it does. Check the pacifier frequently for holes and tears. And remember what we said about strings: Don't tie the pacifier around the child's neck. (For infants and very young children, no toys should have long strings or cords.)

Teethers, rattles, and squeeze toys should also be large enough that they cannot become lodged in

Making a pacifier . . . Not!

If you decide to have your baby use a pacifier, don't make one from a bottle top and nipple, or any other such idea Aunt Polly suggests.

Use only a commercially manufactured pacifier.

the child's mouth. Inspect such items to make sure they won't come apart, allowing a piece to come loose and be swallowed. Because everything goes in the mouth, a parent must keep everything away from the baby that might possibly find its way into her throat. More children have suffocated on uninflated balloons and pieces of balloons than on any other type of toy. This concern is not just for babies in a crib. This is a consideration for every child under 8 years of age. Certainly you won't allow your toddler to blow up balloons, and you'll want to supervise any play with an inflated balloon. When the balloon bursts, immediately discard deflated and broken balloon pieces. Choose Mylar balloons (shiny, metallic) over latex.

Choosing Safe Toys

Any toy you give your child is supposed to be for fun, even if it is also a learning tool. Make sure your child's happy face does not turn into a mask of pain. More than 100,000 children are treated in emergency rooms each year due to toy-related injuries. A few of those children die.

Buy Toys Wisely

You don't have to be an expert to carefully choose toys for your infant or toddler. Here are some simple rules to follow.

- Buy toys that are suitable for the age of your child. This is a safety rule that has nothing to do with the child's intelligence. If the label on the toy says 3 years and older, don't buy it for your 2-year-old. It is likely that these toys have small parts, such as small balls and marbles.

- Read the safety information on the product package. The Child Safety Protection Act prohibits any toy labeled for use by children under age 3 to have any parts that could be ingested or cause choking or aspiration. If you purchase toys from the Internet, be extra cautious. The website may not include product safety warnings, instructions, or age recommendations. In addition, some toys may be manufactured by companies that do not comply with U.S. standards.

- Don't rely solely on the manufacturer. Even if a toy has no warning label, look it over carefully if your child is under 3. Make sure it poses no choking hazard. Does it have small, detachable parts? Does it have small product accessories? How secure are the eyes, nose, and mouth of that stuffed toy you're considering? Make sure stuffed animals and cloth dolls have well-sewn seams. Does it have loose fur or long hair? You don't want fur, hair, pellets or other stuffing to get into your child's mouth.

- Read the labels on all art materials. The Labeling of Hazardous Art Materials Act requires that all art materials must bear this statement of conformance: Conforms to ASTM D-4236. This means the art material has been reviewed by a toxicologist. If any hazardous ingredients have been found, then hazard labeling is required. If the product contains no hazardous materials, there will be no warning, but the statement Conforms to ASTM D-4236 should still be there.

- Don't buy if you don't see a label. These labels are as follows:

  - for fabric products, flame-retardant/flame-resistant

  - for stuffed cloth toys and dolls, washable/hygienic material

  - for electric toys, UL

  - for art materials such as crayons and paint sets, ASTM D-4236. (Do not allow children under 12 to use art materials containing cautionary information.)

  - Only purchase toys labeled non-toxic.

- A small-parts tester/choke tube purchased at a toy store can be used to test items that may present a choking hazard. If the toy itself or a detachable part fits into the choke tube, it is unsafe and should be kept away from children under the age of 3 years and from any child who still puts toys in her mouth.

- Never let your child play with plastic bags and packaging material. These items are not toys, and they present suffocation and choking hazards.

- By this time, you are probably wondering what toys are okay to buy. For guidance, see Chapter 15, "Debra's Holiday Safety Guide," under "Christmas and Chanukah."

Whatever toys you buy, check them frequently for broken, ripped, or loose parts. If they cannot be repaired, promptly discard them. Be familiar with the directions and safe use of every toy in your home.

If you're thinking you never knew toys could be so complicated, don't worry. You'll get the hang of it. It really comes down to good sense, once you've become aware of the essential points.

Avoid Potentially Dangerous Toys

When you think about what toys to avoid, the rules are quite practical.

- Avoid toys with sharp edges and points, electrical toys, and toys with heating elements.

- Avoid battery-operated toys. If you do use toys with batteries (a tape player, for example) make sure the battery compartment has a screw closure.

- Avoid propelled toy darts and other projectiles. They can cause cuts or serious eye injuries.

- Avoid toys that are too noisy. No, this isn't to protect Mom's nerves or Dad's ears. Toys that produce loud noises—such as toy caps, noisemaking guns, or high-volume tape players—can produce sounds at noise levels that can injure a child's hearing. (In addition to the loud noise, caps can ignite, causing burns.) Check the noise level before you buy the toy. This applies to squeaky toys that infants may hold close to their ears. Any loud toy should have directions for safe use—make sure your child follows them.

> **DO IT YOURSELF!**
>
> *Keep all toy information in one place.*
>
> Keep all information and directions about toys in one drawer or file. This would also be a good place to keep warranty information and serial numbers, in case there is a recall.
>
> Stay up to date on recall information.
>
> (Use a similar system for all your juvenile products.)

- Just as you made sure not to hang anything near the baby's crib with a string or ribbon longer than 7 inches, you should continue to avoid toys with strings longer than 7 inches, which can strangle a small child.

- Do not let your baby play with crib toys unsupervised, especially once he begins to push up on his hands and knees.

DO IT YOURSELF!

Make sure the toy box is safe.

When buying or building a toy box, remember: The best toy box will have smooth, finished edges and have either no lid or a light-weight, removable lid.

If you use a hinged lid, make sure it will stay open in any position and won't close unexpectedly. Inspect it periodically to make sure the support device is still working properly.

If you already own a chest with a hinged, freely falling lid, remove the lid or install a spring-loading lid support. Again, make sure it will stay open in any position and won't close unexpectedly, and inspect it periodically.

Just in case your child climbs inside, make sure the chest has plenty of ventilation holes and the lid does not have a latch.

An easy and safe alternative is to store toys on low-set toy shelves or in plastic baskets (no lids).

- Avoid teething toys and other soft plastic toys made of polyvinyl chloride (PVC), which can leach potentially toxic chemicals known as phthalates. Look for products marked as PVC-free or phthalate-free, or contact the manufacturer. (Good news: many manufacturers have stopped using phthalates in teethers, mouthing toys, and other products intended for children under 3.)

Everything in the nursery that is meant for the toddler to use should be kept where he can get to it. (See sidebar above for guidelines in selecting, building, or remodeling a safe toy box.) If you place your toddler's toys or games in a high place—such as the top of the bookcase—you are inviting him to climb. If you have a shelving unit for toys, keep heavy items on the lowest shelf. Show your child how to put toys away in a safe place, where they won't fall or be tripped over. Don't let your infant or toddler have access to an older child's toys.

Now join the fun. Always supervise your child while he is playing; enjoy this wonderful time.

Safe Practices for Baby's Health

Reduce the Risk of Sudden Infant Death Syndrome

All the rules so far have had to do with objects brought into the nursery. There are also a few cautions about what we and other caregivers do with the baby. Sudden infant death syndrome (SIDS) is the sudden, unexplained death of an infant under 1 year of age. It is more common among premature and low birth-weight babies and among twins and triplets. SIDS is more frequent during winter months, and more boys die of SIDS than girls.

Recent studies indicate that there is an abnormality in the brain stems of many SIDS victims that makes them vulnerable to sudden, unexpected deaths. Things that a healthy baby can overcome, such as rebreathing carbon dioxide, overheating, and exposure to secondhand smoke, can be fatal to a baby predisposed with this brain stem abnormality. Currently there is no way to detect this abnormality.

While the cause of SIDS is still not definitive and SIDS may not always be preventable, we can take precautions. Since the beginning of a campaign called "Back to Sleep"—which recommends that babies be placed on their backs and all soft bedding be removed from their cribs—SIDS rates have dropped more than 50 percent.

Here are the guidelines for reducing the likelihood of SIDS:

- Place your baby on her back to sleep at night and naptime. Exception: Some babies have medical conditions that warrant an alternative sleep position. In these instances you should follow your doctor's advice for the best sleep position for your baby.

- Use a firm, tight-fitting mattress in a safety-approved crib or bassinet.

- Remove soft, fluffy, and loose bedding from the sleep area. This includes pillows, blankets, quilts, bumper pads, sheepskins, stuffed toys, and any other soft products. The reason for this is that when the baby sleeps on his tummy or there is soft bedding in or around his sleep area, carbon dioxide (exhaled air) can build up around his head and face. Instead of breathing fresh air, he rebreathes this bad air. Rebreathing carbon dioxide has been identified as a leading cause of sudden infant deaths.

- Use a sleepsack or other type of sleeper as a safe alternative to loose blankets.

- If you do use a blanket, position the baby with her feet at the foot of the crib. Tuck a thin blanket around the crib mattress, only as far as the baby's chest.

- See that the baby's head and face remain uncovered while he is asleep.

- Don't put the baby to sleep on a waterbed, sofa, soft mattress, pillow, or any other soft surface.

DO IT YOURSELF!

Avoid flat spots.

Your baby's skull is soft, and his bones are susceptible to pressure. In addition, if his neck muscles are weak, he is likely to turn his head to the same side most or all the time when he is on his back. Positional plagiocephaly, or flat head, may result. This does not affect the brain, but appearance will be altered.

While this condition is rarely serious, parents can take steps to minimize the potential for flat heads:
- Alternate the direction your baby's head faces when you place him in the crib.

- Because the baby's natural tendency is to look into the room rather than at a wall, the easiest method of counterpositioning is to change his position in the crib. With his head at the head of the crib one time and at the foot of the crib the next, he will turn his head in opposite directions, out into the room.

- If he favors one side or the other in the way he turns his head, regardless of his placement in the crib, move a mobile, toy, or other object of interest (including yourself!) to the opposite side of the room.

- Alternate the arm you use to hold him while feeding.

- One more very important thing! Your baby should have supervised "tummy time" when he begins to be awake several times a day. This is also important for motor development.

A flat spot on the baby's head will usually correct itself once the baby spends more time awake, playing and moving around. But if nothing seems to work, have your baby checked by a doctor—neck stretching exercises may be necessary.

- Don't let your baby overheat during sleep, especially if he already has a fever. Set the room temperature at 68°F to 72°F. At other times, too, keep your baby from being overheated. Promptly remove your baby's outerwear (jacket, sweater, and hat) when indoors, in cars, or in stores.

- Room sharing is safer than sharing your bed with your baby. Experts have serious concerns about potentially hazardous conditions present in the family bed or sofa (such as pillows, comforters, and other bodies). Bed sharing has not been found to be protective against SIDS, but studies suggest that having the crib or other separate sleep surface along side the adult bed or sofa provides greater safety for baby and proximity for parents seeking to facilitate breastfeeding and share closeness with their baby. (Source: First Candle/SIDS Alliance)

- Do not allow smoking anywhere near your baby! Women who smoke cigarettes during or after pregnancy put their babies at increased risk for SIDS. You'll find more information on secondhand smoke in Chapter 11, "Environmental Hazards."

- Educate all caregivers, including your infant's sitter, the personnel at your day-care center, and any relative or friend who may watch your baby. Give them a list of guidelines and stress that you are following the rule about putting your baby to sleep on his back. This is crucial, because research has shown there is an increased risk of SIDS when a baby who routinely sleeps on his back is then put on his stomach to sleep. Continuity of care is a critical component of SIDS risk reduction. Put the baby on his back during nighttime and naptime at home and everywhere else, and make sure others who care for him do the same.

To maximize your baby's health, take her for regular checkups and follow her immunization schedule. If your baby seems ill, contact the pediatrician immediately. Breast-feed your baby; breast milk contains nutrients and antibodies that are needed to help keep your baby healthy. Take preventive measures during pregnancy: do not smoke while pregnant, do not drink alcohol or take any drugs not prescribed for you by your physician after you become pregnant, go for frequent medical checkups, and eat nutritious meals.

This kind of care helps keep your baby from having problems that could put her at risk for SIDS.

There's something else to note in terms of parental behavior: When your baby starts to turn himself over—at about 5 months—you don't have to stay up all night checking on him. Continue to put him down to sleep on his back and get some sleep yourself! SIDS occurs most often in infants 2 to 4 months of age, and 90 percent of SIDS victims are under 6 months of age.

Prevent Shaken Baby Syndrome

Another danger for babies is shaken baby syndrome (SBS). No one should shake a baby, not in anger or in play. SBS may be caused by vigorously shaking an infant by the shoulders, arms, or legs. SBS is more likely to occur when an adult is angry and fun is the farthest thing from anyone's mind. That's why you need your rest!

A baby's neck muscles are too weak to support his head, which is disproportionately large for his body. That's why if he is shaken, his head will flop back and forth, leading to serious injury. In addition, his brain and the blood vessels connecting the skull to the brain are fragile and immature. When a child's head is jerked this way, the brain actually rotates inside the skull cavity, injuring or destroying brain tissue. Blood vessels that feed the brain can also be torn, and when this happens, there is bleeding around the brain. In this circumstance, the blood will pool inside the skull, and that can create even more pressure, lead to further brain damage. Bleeding in the back of the eye (retinal bleeding) is also common in such cases.

A shaken baby can die. Other possible effects range from blindness, spasticity, and seizures to severe motor dysfunction, paralysis, mental retardation, or developmental delays. Children as old as 5 are vulnerable to this type of injury, but babies under 1 year of age are at highest risk.

Whatever the cause, be assured that the baby is not crying to irritate or annoy you. Most of the time you can figure out what the child wants and calm her down by taking care of her immediate needs. After you've tended to the baby's needs, sometimes it is okay to just let her cry. Make sure she's been fed, then check for dirty diapers, and determine the comfort level in the room. After that, put her back into her crib and leave the room. You can still peek in every 10 minutes or so to make sure she's okay, but don't get upset if she continues to cry.

This, too, will pass. It is important to stay calm, because the calmer you are, the calmer your child will be. Sometimes you just have to take a "time-out." Before you lose control, put the baby in her crib and take some time for yourself, away from baby. Some strategies may be helpful here, too; here are some ideas.

- Have a trusted adult watch the child while you take a time-out.

- Build a support system among your friends. Meet them regularly at one another's homes or at a restaurant to complain about how tired all of you are or to talk about your babies. It helps to laugh and cry with others who are going through the same things you are.

- Talk to a friend or relative or someone in your support group. Telephone or chat on the Internet, or just talk over the backyard fence.

> **DO IT YOURSELF!**
>
> *Devise a strategy for calming a crying baby.*
>
> **No special tools required!**
>
> - Soothe the baby by lightly rubbing his back.
> - Rock him in a rocking chair.
> - Give him a pacifier.
> - If he's teething, give him a cool teething ring.
> - Hold him in your arms and sing softly.
> - Take him for a drive in the car or for a ride in the park in his stroller.
> - Contact the pediatrician if sickness is suspected.

- Do something you find relaxing: read, exercise, take a bubble bath, play your favorite music. If scrubbing floors or washing windows does it for you, by all means do it!

Tell everyone you know about the dangers of SIDS and SBS. These are dangers that you can reduce the likelihood of occurring if the people caring for your baby are aware. Tell your relatives and friends and nursery school teachers and babysitters. In other words, your baby will be safe in your nursery only when everyone who enters it is "childproofed."

Be Normal!

In my parenting classes, one point I always make is that parents should try to go about life as normally as possible after the baby has arrived. (Those who already have children will laugh and ask, "What's normal?") The point is that you cannot create a cathedral-like silence around your baby. If you try, you may become neurotic before you learn it won't work. It's unrealistic to think you can keep your home absolutely quiet every time the baby is sleeping—keeping the TV on the lowest volume, whispering softly when talking, turning off the phone ringer.

There may be times when you think you'd do anything to make sure your little darling sleeps as long as possible, but getting him used to silence is the wrong way to do it. If that's what you do, the baby will always require silence every time he sleeps. (Think of having to explain that to his future spouse—that is, if you and your spouse have survived.) Get the baby used to sleeping in the midst of normal background conditions, perhaps a TV on in the next room with a normal volume. Leave the phone's ringer on. If the baby is awakened by a slamming door, it won't be as bad as if the slamming had shattered complete silence.

Review and Safety Checklist

✓ Buy a new crib that meets current safety standards. Look for the Juvenile Products Manufacturers Association certification. Make sure the crib is sturdy, with no loose or missing hardware.

✓ To reduce the risk of sudden infant death syndrome and unintentional suffocation, always lay your baby down to sleep on her back, on a firm, tight-fitting mattress, and remove everything else from her crib.

✓ Never hang anything on or above the crib with a string or ribbon longer than 7 inches. Avoid strings on all infant products, including pacifiers and rattles.

✓ Position any mobile or hanging crib toy out of your child's reach. Remove any hanging crib toys when the baby begins to push up on his hands and knees, or when he is 5 months old, whichever comes first.

✓ Do not place the crib or any other furniture near a window or near blinds or drapery cords.

✓ Buy only toys that are labeled to let you know if it contains small parts and if the toys are appropriate for your child's age. Using a small-parts tester/choke tube will enable you to determine if the toy is a choking hazard.

✓ Never, ever, shake your baby.

Preventing Injuries in the Kitchen

The kitchen is a favorite gathering place for family and close friends, and your baby will learn quite early that this room is a happy, "happening" place. It is up to the parent to make certain all kitchen happenings are, indeed, happy ones. From the very beginning, you'll need to take precautions in the kitchen with your baby, and the number-one rule is this: Never leave your child unsupervised in the kitchen.

By the way, this may be the first room in which your child will hear the word no, so it's a good place to begin teaching her a vocabulary of warning words like hot, sharp, and ouch!

Keeping Baby Away from Danger

Stay Close and Fasten All Safety Restraints

Never leave your child unattended in her high chair. Even when you'll be sitting right beside her, be sure to fasten both the waist and the crotch restraint every time to hold her securely. Don't rely on the feeding tray to restrain or protect her. Without the waist belt and crotch strap holding her securely, she can climb or fall out of the chair or slip between the seat and the tray, possibly getting her head caught and strangling. To prevent a child from slipping down and becoming trapped under the tray, many high chairs sold today are equipped with a passive restraint—a crotch post attached to the tray or seat. Even with that safety feature, however, the safety restraint still must be used every time.

Bring Strangulation Prevention Into the Kitchen

Remember, too, the precautions taken in the nursery regarding things around the neck. Leave a bib on only while you are feeding your baby, then take it off to avoid a strangulation hazard. Try to buy bibs without strings; bibs with Velcro or snaps are a safer choice.

Set Up a Playpen

Keep a playpen (also known as play yard) in the kitchen so your baby can keep you in sight while you prepare food for the family. If you are momentarily distracted, he'll be safe. Get him started in the playpen early by using it instead of the infant seat. Then as months go by, he'll be more likely to play there without protest, even as a curious toddler. This is important, for a toddler can find many ways to get hurt in the kitchen. You can also put the child in his crib or buckle him safely in a high chair in the kitchen. Keep the high chair away from the walls, counters, and table to prevent him from pushing off and tipping the chair over. And be sure to keep all such equipment away from the cooking area!

Keeping Baby Away from What's Hot

Treat the Cooking Area Like a Danger Zone

If range knobs are within reach of your child, take them off when you are not cooking or install stove knob covers or a stove guard. (A little hand can turn the knob, then

DO IT YOURSELF!

Make your cooking area safe.

- Remove stove knobs when not in use.

- Use only back burners.

- Always wear short, tight-fitting sleeves when cooking: loose clothing can catch on fire.

- Keep pot handles facing to the rear and always use a potholder when reaching for handles.

- Never leave cooking foods unattended—this is the number-one cause of house fires.

- Keep towels, potholders, and curtains away from flames and hot surfaces.

- Clean cooking surfaces regularly to prevent grease buildup, which can ignite.

- Install an oven-door lock.

- Reduce a child's temptation to climb on the range or oven by never storing treats or other tantalizing items above any cooking equipment.

- Maintain a no-baby area around the oven.

- Train the family.

touch the hot element.) Gas stoves pose even more danger: when gas is released there is a fire hazard. Use only the back burners on your stove for cooking, and keep handles facing the rear so your child cannot grab them, trying to "help." The oven, too, can be a hazard for a small child. I recommend installing an oven-door lock, so the child can't grab the handle and open it while it is hot. An often ignored danger for young children is the oven door itself. Many ovens get hot enough on the outside to cause burns that require hospitalization. The smallest children, those just learning to walk, are the ones most likely to burn themselves on an oven, especially on their hands. Check your oven to see how hot it gets on the outside. Remember: It takes a long time for an oven to cool.

You may have to train older family members and friends along with your baby. He'll hold up his arms to get out of the playpen, and Grandma will take him out, then walk over to show him the food cooking. If she looks away for a moment, his hand or foot can snare something hot, or he can reach out and touch the oven door.

Keep Hot Food and Beverages Away from Edges

Now that you've told Grandma not to bring the baby to the cooking area, she takes him to the kitchen table where she is having her coffee. Um . . . Grandma? Push the coffee away from the edge of the table, out of his reach. If you set him down on the floor, be sure there is no overhanging tablecloth or mat at the edge of the table. Even with you sitting right there, the baby can reach up, pull the cloth and have hot coffee all over him in a nanosecond. To prevent both of those possibilities, I have two recommendations:

- Invest in spill-resistant mugs to use for hot beverages. Look for a mug that has a spout cover, one that you must actively slide open or press down in order to release the liquid.

- Forego tablecloths and place mats during this period of childhood. (That means less laundry to do—an additional benefit.) All hot foods or beverages, glassware, and utensils should be well away from the edge of kitchen counters or the table.

In addition to taking those precautions, keep children entirely off the floor in the kitchen when anyone is cooking.

Don't Carry Anything Hot While Carrying Your Baby

Even if the hot item is as small as half a cup of coffee, do not carry a child while holding a hot beverage or hot food. Train the rest of the family in this matter, too. You know how a child can wriggle and wiggle. He may choose the exact wrong time to squirm, you'll absently grab for him with the other hand and . . . hot food will be on the baby instantly.

Precautions with the Microwave Oven

There are other ways for a baby to be burned in the kitchen. You know how much it hurts when you sip coffee that's too hot. You don't want that to happen to your child! The greatest danger of offering food that is too hot occurs when it has been heated in the microwave oven. Something may feel cool at the edge but have hot spots in the middle or bottom. That's why I highly recommend that you avoid or use extreme caution while warming up anything in the microwave for your child.

Never Heat a Bottle in the Microwave

A bottle warmed in the microwave heats unevenly and—even after shaking and even though the bottle may feel cool—there can be hot spots in the milk that could burn your baby's mouth and throat. The best way to warm your baby's bottle from the refrigerator is to place it in a pan of hot (not boiling) water for a few minutes. Then shake and test the temperature by squirting a few drops on your inner wrist. It should feel comfortable—barely warm. Although your baby may seem to prefer it, there really is no health reason to feed her a warmed bottle. In fact, if she becomes accustomed to drinking bottles slightly cold or at room temperature, you'll be saved the time and hassle of heating it and be able to feed her right away, especially when she is crying to be fed.

Avoid Heating Certain Baby Foods in the Microwave

Do not use the microwave to heat baby food containing meats, meat sticks, or eggs. These foods tend to build up hot spots and splatter when the door of the microwave is opened. You or your baby could be seriously burned.

Don't Take Shortcuts

The microwave makes quick work of heating anything, but sometimes you'll be tempted to take an additional shortcut without thinking about the potential danger. This might happen, for example, when you intend to heat commercially prepared baby food the "quickest" way. Never heat solid baby food in the jar it came in. The center will heat to dangerously high temperatures while food in other parts of the jar will stay cool. Before heating, transfer the food to a dish. A 4-ounce dish of solid food cooked on high power will take approximately 15 seconds. Before serving any microwaved food, stir it well with a spoon or fork, then let it stand—30 seconds for that 4-ounce helping of baby food. You cannot tell how hot an item is just by touching the outside of the container, so taste-test the food to see if it's lukewarm, the proper serving temperature. Don't use the same spoon to test the food that will be used to feed your baby. Even your saliva contains bacteria and viruses.

When using the microwave for heating any food, do not use takeout or cold-storage containers like margarine tubs. Such material can warp or melt in contact with hot food, allowing chemicals from the plastic to get into the food. Avoid this by using only glass or lead-free ceramic cookware approved for microwave ovens.

Don't Let Your Child "Help"

Taking food from the microwave is not an appropriate helping chore for a child. Don't even let her remove coverings or lids from food you have cooked in the microwave—it's dangerous.

Preventing Injuries Before They Happen

Install Safety Latches

Prevention is the watchword elsewhere in the kitchen, too. Cabinets are awfully enticing to a climbing toddler. Up there is where all the good stuff is kept! No matter how vigilant we try to be, sometimes the little rascal gets a step ahead of us. On the high cabinets as well as those on the floor, install devices that keep the door closed beneath a child's tug but allow it to open easily under the pull an adult can exert. Store knives and other sharp utensils in drawers or cabinets secured with safety latches. Install an appliance lock on your refrigerator, too. Raw meat, as well as medications such as antibiotics, is stored there. One appliance that comes with a lock is the dishwasher. Keep it locked, but just in case, make sure forks and knives are pointed downward.

While you don't want a child under 3 years old to think of a cooking pan as a toy (not knowing the difference when it is full of something hot), some things in the cabinets are not harmful. It won't hurt if the child plays with a wooden spoon and an empty storage container. (Mom and Dad may need earplugs, but that's another matter.) But falling cans can cause a bruise, or worse, and a knife stored on a door or in a drawer can draw blood before you can turn around. There are other dangers lurking behind those cabinet doors as well, such as products that help us keep the kitchen clean or rid the house of insects and other

pests. A "poison patrol" will be discussed at length in Chapter 10, "Common Poisons in the Home." Some poisons are look-alikes for good things one eats or drinks, so don't give your toddler a chance to make a fatal mistake.

Stash the Trash

Kitchen trash can contain hazardous objects, as well as spoiled food. Recycling bins also hold potentially hazardous glass and aluminum can lids. Keep the trash and recycling containers securely closed and out of your child's sight and reach.

Keep the Step Stool Inaccessible to Young Children

A step stool is a handy thing to have in the kitchen, but you don't want your child to climb up on it . . . the better to reach something that's dangerous for her to have. When you purchase your step stool, look for one with a handrail that enables you to hold onto it while standing on the top step. Keep it handy for yourself, but not for your child.

Review and Safety Checklist

✓ Don't leave your baby unattended in an infant seat or high chair; buckle up for safety.

✓ Always keep a child away from the cooking area while you are cooking. Keep a playpen in the kitchen for your baby's freedom of movement and your own peace of mind. But remain watchful! Never leave your baby unattended, even in the playpen.

✓ Remove the range knobs when you are not cooking. Use the back burners whenever possible. Turn pot handles to the back.

✓ Place all hot dishes and beverages, glassware, and utensils in the middle of the table, out of your child's reach. Avoid using place mats and tablecloths.

✓ Don't carry your baby and hot food or beverages at the same time.

✓ Never heat a bottle in the microwave. Before offering microwave-heated food to your child, stir it well, let stand, then taste it to make sure it is only lukewarm.

✓ To keep your baby from opening kitchen cabinets, install safety devices or strong rubber bands around knobs.

✓ Securely lock poisonous and hazardous products you keep in the kitchen out of sight and reach of children.

More about the Kitchen

Keeping Your Baby's Food Safe

Now that you know how to keep your kitchen safe, consider another important thing about the kitchen: food. In the beginning, you'll be breast-feeding or preparing formula. Then you will introduce special baby food (either commercial or homemade) to your child. Later, many foods she eats will be taken from the fare offered to the entire family. When your baby begins to eat solids, she will depend on you to give her food that will not choke her or make her sick.

We'll look at baby food first, then discuss tap-water safety, which is quite important when you are using water to prepare formula or food for your baby. After that we'll discuss ways to decrease the risk of food allergies and practices for avoiding food-borne illness.

Baby Food Basics

Keeping your baby's food safe is an important part of keeping the baby herself safe. From the time you prepare or purchase a food product until you store it and eventually feed it to your little darling, you will want to take great care.

Pay Attention to the Package

The first precaution you'll take is at the store. Check the use by date on any product your baby will ingest; if the date has passed, don't buy it. Check again when you remove baby food, juice, or formula from your cabinet to give to your baby. If the expiration date has passed, don't use it. Wash the lid before opening, then listen for the pop. If the lid of the baby food jar doesn't pop, it has not been sealed safely, so don't use it. After opening, check for chipped glass or rusty lids. If you see any such defect, do not use the product.

Learn What and How to Feed Your Baby to Encourage Good Health

Ask your pediatrician for any feeding guidelines you should follow specifically for your baby, and inquire about any possible need to use bottled water or sterilized water when mixing formula. No matter how or what you feed him, always wash your hands thoroughly before beginning food or formula preparation. There are other general guidelines for feeding him:

- When mixing water and formula, carefully follow the manufacturer's recommendations. For the first year of life a baby should drink breast milk or formula, not cow's milk. If you give your child between 1 and 2 years of age cow's milk, it should be whole milk. Neither skim milk nor low-fat milk is recommended for a child below the age of 2.

- You may introduce solid food to your 4-to-6-month-old baby.

- Use caution when warming up food or beverages for your baby. Set the bottle of formula, expressed breast milk, or other liquid into a pan of hot—not boiling—water for a few minutes. Do not use the microwave (see the section "Precautions with the Microwave Oven" in Chapter 2 for a more thorough discussion). In addition, you should not use the microwave to heat meats, meat sticks, eggs, or jars of food. Hot spots created in the microwave can burn your baby's mouth.

- Test before feeding. Always shake the bottle and test the temperature by dropping some of the beverage on your inner wrist. After stirring food thoroughly, test it by tasting it to see if it's lukewarm. Remember: Don't use the testing spoon to feed your baby; your saliva contains bacteria and viruses that could harm your child.

- Unless you know for sure all the food will be eaten in the first sitting, do not feed your baby directly from the jar. Put a small amount in a clean bowl and feed your child from that bowl. After feeding, discard any leftovers remaining in the bowl, jar, or bottle. Bacteria from the baby's saliva can grow and multiply; neither refrigerating nor reheating will prevent or destroy the contaminants.

- Be sure containers are clean. Prior to first use, sterilize new bottles, nipples, and rings. After each use, clean reusable bottles, caps, nipples, and other utensils by washing them in a dishwasher or in hot tap water with dishwashing liquid; rinse in hot water. If your water is from a well or is not chlorinated, you should sterilize utensils before use.

Store Baby Food Safely

Store unopened baby food and formula in a dry, cool area. Read the label to see if there are special storage recommendations. Leftovers may be refrigerated or frozen. Once opened, baby food (solids or liquids) should not be left at room temperature for more than an hour. (The guideline for food safety is usually 2 hours, but with infant food—for safety's sake—many experts recommend reducing that time to 1 hour.) When you store food or liquids that have been opened, don't trust your memory. Label the container with the date the product was originally opened.

Freezing leftover formula is not recommended, but it can be refrigerated for 2 days. Don't let it stand in an open container; keep it covered. Store unused baby food in the original jar with a tightly closed lid. To know whether a particular product can be frozen, you will read the manufacturer's recommendation on the label, of course, but there are some general guidelines for time limits for refrigerating or freezing baby food products:

- Strained fruits and vegetables: refrigerate for 2 to 3 days, freeze for 6 to 8 months

- Strained meats and eggs: refrigerate for 1 day, freeze for 1 to 2 months

- Meat/vegetable combinations: refrigerate for 1 to 2 days, freeze for 1 to 2 months

- Homemade baby foods: refrigerate for 1 to 2 days, freeze for 3 to 4 months

You'll want to take care of the milk you hand express or pump as carefully as you handle other baby food. See Appendix F, "Storing Human Milk," for guidelines on safe handling of your milk.

Tap Water Safety

Infants drink more fluids per pound of body weight than anyone else in the family, so parents are right to be concerned about the safety of their tap water. This worry is particularly apt because the immature system of an infant makes the baby especially vulnerable to microbial contaminants sometimes found in tap water.

In general, there is no need for alarm in the United States, due largely to the Safe Drinking Water Act of 1974 and its amendments (passed in 1986 and 1996). As a consequence of the Act, the EPA has issued primary drinking water standards called Maximum Contaminant Levels for about 90 contaminants. These standards limit the amount of each substance allowed to be present in drinking water. United States public water suppliers are required to perform water-quality monitoring to ensure that the water remains free from unsafe levels of contamination. Utilities must notify customers when tests show the water does not meet EPA standards.

The EPA has also issued secondary drinking water standards concerning the taste, odor, color, and certain other aesthetic qualities of drinking water that, although they may be undesirable, are not considered to pose a health risk. The EPA recommends these guidelines as reasonable goals, but states are not legally required to comply. However, some states have adopted their own enforceable regulations.

You can be more at risk for contaminants in your water if it comes from a private water supply or from a smaller water system that may not have enough funds to hire trained specialists or make necessary improvements. Private water supplies are defined as domestic systems serving homes supplied by individual wells.

These are not regulated under the Safe Drinking Water Act. Individual homeowners in these situations must take steps on their own to test and treat their water as necessary, to avoid any possible serious health effects.

It is no overstatement to affix the label enemy to the bacteria, parasites, nitrates, trihalomethanes, arsenic, radon, lead, and pesticides that may be lurking in your water. Any of them can potentially harm your baby.

Learn about Contaminants Sometimes Found in Drinking Water

Microbial Pathogens (Bacteria and Parasites)

These contaminants (cryptosporidia and giardia, for example) are common in lakes and rivers contaminated with human and animal fecal waste. They can cause diarrhea, nausea, and stomach cramps, and they are most dangerous for infants, the elderly, and immune-compromised adults. Pregnant women should take the following precautions as well.

- Boil the water. The best way to kill these contaminants is to boil the water. Bring the water to a rolling boil for 1 minute, remove it from the heat source, and let it cool before serving. Remember to also boil water that will be used for ice cubes.

- Filter the water. Essentially there are two kinds of filters, based on where the device is to be located. A point-of-use system treats water at a single tap; a point-of-entry system treats water that will be used throughout the home. When you make your purchase, look for a label that says the device is equipped with an Absolute 1-micrometer filter or is certified by NSF International under Standard 53 for Cyst Removal. (Note: This filter may not protect you from organisms smaller than cryptosporidia.) Utilities must filter out giardia and cryptosporidia if present.

Nitrates

A high nitrate level is likely to be found in rural areas where ground and surface water is contaminated with animal waste or runoff from nitrogen-based fertilizer. Infants are most at risk because nitrates reacting with the hemoglobin in the baby's blood produce an anemic condition known as blue baby. Left untreated, the condition can be fatal. Unless you know your water is safe, do not drink the water if you are pregnant. And don't give your baby any nitrate-contaminated water or food, or formula that contains nitrate-contaminated water. Boiling does not help. In fact, prolonged boiling of water contaminated by this element increases the nitrate concentration. Either buy bottled water from a quality source or invest in a home treatment device.

Important Note: Do not feed home-prepared spinach, beets, turnips, carrots, or collard greens to your baby. These home-prepared vegetables may contain large amounts of nitrates. Buy commercially prepared jars of these foods; baby food companies prepare foods only from crops found to have lower nitrate levels.

Trihalomethanes (THMs)

When chlorine—the chemical used to disinfect water—combines with naturally occurring organic matter like decaying leaves, THMs are formed. Linked to bladder and rectal cancer, THMs may cause the most risk for fetuses. One study involving more than 5,000 women found that women who, each day, drank 5 or more glasses of cold tap water containing at least 75 parts per billion (ppb) of THMs were at greater risk of miscarriage than women with less exposure. The current federal level for THM is 80 ppb. If you are pregnant, err on the side of safety. Don't drink water that contains consistent THM levels at or above 75 ppb. Use a carbon-activated filter to lower THM or drink bottled water. Because one can also inhale THM, reduce your shower time and have good ventilation in your bathroom.

Arsenic

This contaminant has been linked to cancer, skin lesions, endocrine disruption, and nerve damage. In 2001, the EPA revised the Maximum Contaminant Level for arsenic in drinking water to 10 ppb. Water systems must meet this new standard by January 2006.

Test for Other Toxic Contaminants

Radon, lead, and pesticides can also contaminate drinking water. For a thorough discussion of specific risks associated with these elements and the best ways to test and treat for them, please refer to Chapter 11, "Environmental Hazards."

Radon, a radioactive gas, can seep into ground water, and your family can be exposed to it not only through drinking water, but also by showering or washing dishes. However, indoor air pollution by radon is usually more of a health concern.

For a thorough discussion about lead, please refer to the section "Lead" in Chapter 11, "Environmental Hazards."

Pesticides (including herbicides, insecticides, and fungicides) pose more risk for families living in active farming communities.

Investigate Your Water Supply

If you are on a public water system, contact your local water utility. You'll find the phone number on your water bill. Ask the following three questions:

1. Where does my drinking water come from?

2. How is this water treated?

3. What contaminants are tested?

Then ask for a copy of the utility's most current Drinking Water Contaminant Analysis Report. The law requires all community water systems to furnish this information to you in an annual Consumer Confidence Report by July 1 for the previous calendar year. This report may also be available online at www.epa.gov/safewater/dwinfo.htm or at your local library. Take particular note of any violations.

Also call your state's Health Department and Department of Environmental Protection to ask what contaminants they test for and request copies of their analysis reports. The reports cannot tell you what happens to your water between the treatment plant and your tap. You will need to have your own water tested for lead and copper. If your water has a blue-green tinge or if your fixtures are stained blue-green, you should suspect high copper levels.

Heed the Safety Guidelines If You Are on a Private Water System

Call your state and local health departments or your local cooperative extension agent. Ask about groundwater problems in your area and inquire about past, present, or potential problems.

Ask about testing. Some local health departments test water for free; some do so for a fee. You can also contact your state laboratory certification office for a listing of certified drinking water laboratories in your state. The EPA recommends annual testing for nitrates, total dissolved solids and coliform bacteria, which, though generally harmless, may indicate other contamination. If a problem is suspected, you may need to test more frequently and for more potential contaminants. Well water should also be tested for lead. Testing for lead is particularly important if you have lead pipes, soldered copper joints, or brass parts in the pump.

Additional testing is indicated if any of these conditions or activities is present or nearby: intensive agriculture, a dump, a landfill, a factory, a gasoline service station, or a dry-cleaning operation. Ask your local health department and your cooperative extension agent for guidance on what specific contaminants should be tested for.

Test Your Water

You should have your water tested by a state-certified laboratory. To get the names of certified labs nearest you, call your state laboratory certification office or, if you prefer, call the EPA Safe Drinking Water Hotline: (800) 426-4791.

To be on the safe side, do not have your water tested by a company trying to sell you a water treatment device. If the results from their lab indicate you do have a serious problem, get a second opinion from a different lab before spending money on an expensive water treatment product.

Find the Right Water Treatment for Your Family

Do your homework! There is a wide range of prices; don't buy more than you need. If a $20 pitcher will do the job necessary to protect the tap water in your home, why buy an under-the-sink unit that costs $1,000?

There is no federal agency that tests or approves home water treatment devices nor can one device eliminate every kind of drinking water contaminant. To find a quality product and one that is certified to remove the specific contaminants found in your drinking water, you can choose between two agencies:

- NSF International is an independent, not-for-profit organization that tests and certifies home water treatment units for health-related contaminants and aesthetic effects. Contact them by phone, (800) 673-8010, or visit their website, www.nsf.org.

- The Water Quality Association is an independent, not-for-profit organization that classifies units according to the contaminants they remove. It also lists units that have earned its approval. Note that the association does not test or evaluate units for health-related contaminants, only for aesthetic effects such as hardness and chlorine. Visit their website at www.wqa.org.

Follow the Manufacturer's Instructions for Maintenance or Get a Maintenance Contract

Any product requires periodic maintenance or replacement. The unit that insures the purity of your water is no exception. In fact, a filter that is poorly maintained can be worse for your health than drinking the water without the filter. A dirty filter can be a breeding ground for bacteria, and it can cause contaminants to begin flowing back into the water.

Knowing yourself is important. Can you—and will you—follow instructions for proper maintenance? If you are not so inclined, it is best to purchase a contract from the dealer.

Comparison-Shop If Bottled Water Is Your Choice

The FDA regulates bottled water as a food. It imposes quality standards equivalent to the EPA's drinking water standards. Treat bottled water as you do foods; refrigerate after opening. Whether bottled water is any safer than the water from your tap can be disputed. In fact, some bottled water is simply repackaged municipal water. The source of the water and the practices of the company selling it can cause quality to vary. Contact the manufacturer of your favorite brand, ask how they treat their water, and request a copy of their most recent water analysis. The International Bottled Water Association represents the bottled water industry. You can contact them by calling (800) WATER-11 or by visiting their website, www.bottledwater.org. NSF International also provides testing and certification of bottled water (see contact information in Section 6, above). Drinking bottled water or using an in-house treatment system is a temporary solution. The underlying problem remains. Actively support efforts to upgrade the supply and treatment of safe drinking water and to protect water supplies from industrial and agricultural pollution. And do your part at home compost, recycle, and properly dispose of hazardous material.

Foods That Can Choke

Consider the size and texture of any food before giving it to your baby. Do not allow children under age 6 to eat hard, round foods, including hot dogs. Trust yourself. If you have any doubt about whether a food is safe for your child, don't serve it. Even with all the precautions considered below, a small piece of food may lodge in a child's throat. This point cannot be made too often: Take an infant/child CPR and first aid course.

Know What Not to Serve

These foods can choke your child: popcorn, nuts, seeds, whole grapes, apple chunks, raisins, raw carrots and celery, hard candies, hot dogs. In addition, sticky food can cause your child to choke. Never spoon-feed peanut butter to your child. If you do serve it, put a thin layer of it on a sandwich, and always serve it with a beverage.

Prepare Food So It Won't Choke Your Child

Any round or cylindrical objects can fit snugly in the windpipe, completely blocking the flow of air. This is as true for food as anything else, so don't cut vegetables in circles. Instead, cut vegetables into small strips. Vegetables may need to be cooked or steamed to soften them. Cut or break any food into small, angular pieces so they can't lodge in your child's throat. Before giving fruit or vegetables to the child, remove pits, skin, and seeds. To be extra safe, you may wish to use a food processor or blender to puree table foods so they're soft enough for your baby to chew. If you feed a hot dog to a child under 6 years of age, make sure you remove the peel and slice it lengthwise, then cut it in small, bite-size pieces.

Use Caution Away From Home

When you take your baby to a restaurant, be alert from the moment you walk in. At the table, be especially alert if adult munchies—freebies like peanuts and popcorn—are part of the fare. These should be kept out of your baby's reach. Even food you've ordered may cause a toddler to choke, especially if he's so hungry he shovels the food into his mouth. Before he gets his hands on it, cut the food into bite-size pieces, and if he's within reach of your plate, cut up your food, too. On the way out of the restaurant or any other business where impulse items are displayed at the checkout station, watch your baby's hands. He can grab hard candy or any other small item and have it in his mouth before you notice.

When you travel with your child in a car, avoid feeding him, or be sure he eats only soft foods. An unexpected bump or swerve could make him choke. If the driver is the only adult in the car, it may be impossible to attend to the child quickly.

Teach Table Manners for Safety

Good manners at the table make eating safer. Teach your child to sit upright, eat slowly, take small bites, and chew each bite thoroughly. Always supervise your child's mealtime to make sure she understands and follows the rules. Eating should always take place while sitting. Walking, running, or playing should not accompany eating; neither should talking, laughing, or giggling. Eating is not a multitasking endeavor. Enjoying a meal is good for the digestion and disposition, but fun at the cost of safety is a no-no.

Start early with being careful about how your baby eats. An infant should never have his bottle propped up. Hold your baby during bottle feeding. Hold the baby in a semi-upright position and angle the bottle accordingly. I mentioned this in Chapter 1, but it bears repeating. Not only is this a special bonding, snuggle time, it also lessens the risk of choking. Drinking from a propped bottle can lead to tooth decay and ear infections, as well. So don't prop!

Allergies: Know What Foods to Avoid

If you or your spouse has a family history of allergies—to animals, dust, pollen, or foods—your child may be at an increased risk for developing allergies. In order to prevent or delay the onset of food allergy in your child, your pediatrician may recommend that you wait to start solid foods until age 6 months. Your child should be older than a year old before you introduce dairy products, more than 2 years old for eggs and more than 3 years old for peanuts, nuts, fish, and seafood. (Remember the choking hazard we just discussed: No whole peanuts or other nuts for your child until she is 6!) Consult with your pediatrician about which food is appropriate at which age. The theory is that delaying the introduction of these highly allergenic foods may allow the child's immune system to mature and therefore the child will not develop allergies to them. If you are pregnant or are breast-feeding, you may have to eliminate certain foods from your diet. Your doctor and the pediatrician can, based on family history, help you decide which foods to avoid.

What You Need to Know about Food-Borne Illness

Food-borne illness is not just a problem found in other parts of the world. In fact, according to the Centers for Disease Control and Prevention, 76 million Americans get sick and 5,000 die from food-borne illnesses each year. Infants and children are more at risk because they have less-developed immune systems. Common symptoms include diarrhea, abdominal cramping, fever, blood, or pus in the stool, headache, vomiting, and severe exhaustion. In a child, these symptoms must be treated immediately because such illness can be life-threatening.

Be aware that, although symptoms may appear as early as half an hour after the contaminated food is consumed, they may not develop for several days or weeks. When trying to nail down the cause of symptoms, don't just look back over 1 or 2 days.

Know What Foods to Avoid

Some foods are more likely than others to be contaminated with harmful bacteria. Children, pregnant women, immunocompromised persons, and the elderly should avoid the following foods:

- Soft, unprocessed cheeses. Soft cheese made from unpasteurized milk—such as feta, Camembert, blue-veined cheeses, and Mexican-style cheeses—can harbor bacteria of the genus Listeria. In babies it can cause a brain infection that can lead to brain damage; in pregnant woman it can cause miscarriages and stillbirths. Cheddar and other hard cheeses, cottage cheese, processed cheeses, and cream cheese are okay to eat.

- *Raw or undercooked eggs or products made with raw or undercooked eggs.* Egg dishes should be cooked to a temperature of 160°F or by a visual check, with both the yolk and white firm, not runny. Hard-cooked eggs should be safe for everyone in the family to eat. Do not give your children soft-cooked or runny eggs. Don't use recipes in which eggs remain raw or only partially cooked, such as homemade ice cream, mayonnaise, Caesar salad dressing, or French toast.

- *Don't eat cookie dough either.* (I can hear you groaning.) We're talking about the homemade batter that's made with raw eggs, which can be contaminated with Salmonella. My words of wisdom: Eat your homemade cookies cooked.

- *Raw or undercooked meat, poultry, fish, and shellfish.* Foods from animals, such as meat, poultry, fish, and shellfish, when eaten raw or undercooked, can contain life-threatening bacteria and viruses. Children, pregnant women, immunocompromised persons, and the elderly should not eat or sample raw fish or shellfish such as oysters, shrimp, crab, clams, sushi, or sashimi. Nor should they eat meat or seafood ordered undercooked, such as rare hamburger, beef, lamb, pork, or fish. Always use a food thermometer to be sure foods are safely cooked. (See page 45 for a temperature table.)

- *Raw sprouts, such as alfalfa, clover, or radish.* These have been associated with Salmonella and E. coli 0157:H7. Cook sprouts thoroughly to kill off the bacteria.

- *Unpasteurized milk, juice, or cider.* These can contain bacteria, including E. coli 0157:H7 and Salmonella. Pasteurization is a heat process that destroys harmful levels of bacteria in liquids. Pasteurized products include shelf-stable items such as those packaged in cans, bottles, and juice boxes, and found unrefrigerated in the grocery store. Concentrated juice and juice from concentrate are also pasteurized. Warning: Some fresh juices and ciders—commonly sold at roadside stands, country fairs, and juice bars, as well as those kept on ice or in refrigerated display cases at grocery stores—are unpasteurized. Always check for labeling information on juice packages. When in doubt, ask. If you have purchased a product and are unsure whether it has been pasteurized, bring it to a boil for a minute, then cool before drinking it or giving it to your child to drink.

Take Care with Fruits and Vegetables

It may surprise you to learn that fresh fruits and vegetables can harbor disease-causing bacteria. How can this happen? The answer lies at a number of points along the route the food takes to get to your table from the field: a) fertilization with raw manure, b) irrigation with contaminated water, c) rinsing the plants with contaminated water, and d) contamination by food handlers. Before offering any raw produce to your family, it should be thoroughly washed under clean running water. This is true even for organic fruits and vegetables, and even if the label says the produce has already been washed. If appropriate, use a small scrub brush. Wash and scrub produce that has a rind, too, such as cantaloupe and pineapple, because pathogens on the outside of the rind can contaminate the inside when you cut it. When you're washing lettuce and other leafy vegetables, discard the outer leaves. Separate the inner leaves and wash thoroughly.

Know When to Avoid Mushrooms and Honey

Wild Mushrooms

Some common species of wild mushrooms are capable of causing poisoning or even death. Only an expert with specialized training can distinguish the edible kinds from the others. Eat only mushrooms you've purchased in the grocery store or the ones you've raised at home from cultures bought from reputable sources.

Honey

Do not serve honey to children under age 1. It may surprise you to learn that honey should never be given to a baby. This food—healthful for most of us—may contain bacterial spores that can cause infant botulism, a rare but serious disease that affects the nervous system of young babies. Don't add honey to your baby's food, water, or formula, and don't dip your baby's pacifier in honey.

Follow Guidelines for Safe Food Handling

Shop Carefully

- Go to reputable stores that are clean and well maintained and that have meat and poultry supplied by USDA-inspected or state-inspected plants. Fish should be purchased at markets where supplies are bought from state-approved sources.

- Carefully consider what you put in your shopping cart. Do not purchase foods beyond the sell by or use by dates.

- Do not choose foods with torn or broken packaging. Do not buy cans or glass jars with dents, cracks, or bulging lids—this can be a sign that the food contains harmful microorganisms.

- Buy only meat, poultry, or seafood that has been refrigerated or frozen. Place these foods in plastic bags to keep juices from leaking out.

- Look for grade A or AA refrigerated eggs with clean, uncracked shells.

- Select fruits and vegetables that are free of mold and decay. Make sure the produce isn't brownish, slimy, dried-out, or damaged.

Store Food the Right Way

- Choose perishable foods last—right before grocery checkout—then go straight home and refrigerate or freeze the food immediately. If you have other errands, do them before shopping for perishable food.

- Use an appliance thermometer to be sure the refrigerator is 40°F or lower and that the freezer is 0°F to keep food at safe temperatures.

- Store canned goods in a cool, dry place for use within 18 months. Never put them above the stove, under the sink, or in a garage or damp basement.

- Most fruits and vegetables should be stored in the refrigerator, but apples and bananas may be stored on your countertop. Potatoes and onions can also be stored at room temperature, but in a cool, dry place. Don't put them under the sink, because leakage from pipes can damage food.

Thaw with Safety in Mind

Do not thaw food on the counter! Bacteria multiply quickly at room temperature. The following are safe options.

- Defrost food in the refrigerator. This requires planning ahead because several hours are required.

- Put the food in a watertight plastic bag and immerse in cold water; change the water every 30 minutes.

- Use the microwave. Follow the manufacturer's directions for your microwave model. Foods defrosted by this method should be cooked right away.

Keep Everything Clean When Preparing Food

Wash your hands with soap and warm water for at least 20 seconds—and use a nail brush—before and after handling food or food utensils. Clean the counters, tables, cutting boards, and utensils thoroughly with hot, soapy water after use and before using them on another food. When sanitizing (which should be done often), use a solution of 1 teaspoon chlorine bleach per quart of water. Wash the lids of canned foods and drinks before opening to keep dirt from

---

Hand Washing 101

- Wet your hands under warm running water.

- Apply a mild liquid soap or clean bar soap.

- Rub your hands together vigorously until a soapy lather appears. Continue for at least 20 seconds. (Hint: It takes about 20 seconds to sing the alphabet song.)

- Scrub under the fingernails, between fingers, and around the tops and palms of the hands.

- Rinse thoroughly under warm running water.

- Dry hands with a clean, dry towel or paper towel.

- Teach your toddler how to wash his hands. Make it fun by singing a song (such as the alphabet song) and add your own words while you dry your hands together.

getting into the food. Clean the blade of the can opener frequently. Even if you're trying to save the planet by limiting the use of throwaway products, I highly recommend that you consider using paper towels to clean up all kitchen surfaces, especially those touched by raw meat, poultry, or seafood juices. Harmful bacteria multiply quickly on kitchen towels, sponges, and cloths. If you choose to use cloth items, wash them often in the hot water cycle of your washing machine. If you choose to use sponges, discard them often.

Cook Food Thoroughly

Always use a properly calibrated analog or digital food thermometer to be sure foods are safely cooked. Thermometers are inexpensive and easy to use; just follow the instructions and make sure you have the right kind for the job you're doing. Don't think you can tell by looking whether meat is cooked well enough. Your child's hamburger must be cooked to an internal temperature of at least 160°F. It is important to always use a thermometer because hamburgers can turn prematurely brown before reaching a safe temperature. When reheating leftovers, heat to 165°F. Ready-to-eat food such as hot dogs and cold cuts should be heated until they are steaming hot. Here's a temperature table:

Food	Minimum Temperature	Comment
Ground meat	160° F	
Whole chicken or turkey	180° F	measured in the thigh
Breasts and roasts	170° F	
Fish	160° F	flakes easily with a fork
Eggs	160° F	yolks and whites are firm

Please remember that color does not reliably indicate whether ground beef patties have been cooked to a temperature high enough to kill *E. coli* O157:H7, a potentially deadly bacteria. **Important note:** Hemolytic uremic syndrome may develop as a result of *E. coli* O157:H7 consumption, particularly in very young children. This syndrome can cause permanent kidney damage or failure, possibly resulting in death. Be aware that studies suggest that antibiotic treatment of children with *E. coli* O157:H7 infection increases the risk of the Hemolytic uremic syndrome.

Serve and Handle Food Carefully

- Perishable foods. Never leave perishable food at room temperature for more than 2 hours. This includes raw and cooked meat, poultry, and seafood products. Once fruits and vegetables are cut, it is safest to also limit their time at

When to Wash Hands

Before . . .
- preparing bottles or feeding children
- giving or applying medication to child or self
- preparing food
- eating

After . . .
- preparing food
- eating
- using the bathroom
- assisting child in using toilet
- changing diapers (wash baby's hands, too!)
- blowing one's nose
- covering a sneeze
- wiping child's runny nose
- cleaning up spit, vomit, or similar substances
- handling pets, pet cages, or other pet objects
- handling animal waste
- engaging in outdoor activities
- handling trash
- cleaning the house
- working or gardening outdoors
- removing gloves used for any purpose

Other times . . .
- when hands are visibly dirty
- when someone in the house is sick, wash hands more often

room temperature. If perishable food is left at room temperature for more than 2 hours, bacteria can grow to harmful levels.

- Leftovers. All leftovers should be handled with care. Any marinade used on raw meat, fish, or poultry should never be reused; toss it out. If it is a hot day (90°F or above), refrigerate leftovers within an hour. You can stretch the time to 2 hours on a cool day or in an air-conditioned house. When refrigerating, divide the leftovers into shallow, covered containers so the food will chill rapidly and evenly.

Know when you should not cook. If you have an infected sore or cut or have been sick with vomiting or diarrhea, do not prepare or handle food. The germs that are making you sick can easily be passed to your family, and your baby is the most at risk.

Reduce the Risk of Pesticides in Your Child's Diet

Our children may be exposed to pesticides from residues found in their food. Although pesticides are discussed in greater detail in Chapter 11, "Environmental Hazards," I'll quickly mention here some ways you can reduce the risk of pesticide residues in your child's diet.

When Possible, Go Organic

You may choose to purchase foods and beverages that are certified as organically grown and processed. Organic food is produced according to certifiable guidelines, using renewable resources and conserving soil and water. For animal products, antibiotics and growth hormones are restricted. For fruits, vegetables, and grains, restrictions pertain for most conventional pesticides, petroleum- or sewage-sludge-based fertilizers, bioengineering, and ionizing radiation.

Before a product can be labeled organic, a government-approved certifier inspects the farm where the food is grown to make sure the farmer is following all the rules necessary to meet USDA organic standards. Companies that handle or process organic food must be certified as well. Today, many groceries carry organic food, but you can also grow your own chemical-free produce in your backyard. When you grow your own, you have more control over your food. This can be a great family activity.

Lower Pesticide Risk in Other Foods

- Choose a variety of foods. This will give your family a better mix of nutrients and reduce the likelihood of exposure to a single pesticide.

- Trim the fat from meat and poultry. Pesticides tend to accumulate in the fatty tissues of animals.

- Remove the skin from chicken and fish.

- Discard the fat in broths and pan drippings.

- Buy produce in season. Not only is it less expensive, but it is also less likely to have been treated with fungicides and other preservatives.

- Buy from local growers. In this way you avoid buying food shipped over long distances or stored over long periods of time. Not only can you quiz the producer on the farming methods used, you will also be giving support to the local farmer.

- Wash produce under clean running water, which has an abrasive effect. Thoroughly scrub produce with a soft brush. Be aware the scrubbing will not remove pesticide residues that have been absorbed into the produce before harvest. It is recommended that you not wash produce with household soap because soap residues are very difficult to completely rinse off, and most soaps are not meant to be consumed.

- Peel skin or outer leaves.

Limit Exposure to Mercury in Fish

Fish and shellfish can be important parts of a healthy and balanced diet. They are good sources of high quality protein and other essential nutrients. However, some fish contain mercury and can be harmful to a young child or unborn baby. Women who are planning to become pregnant, those who are pregnant or nursing, and those who prepare meals for a young child should take care.

Mercury is a metal found naturally in the environment. Whether from natural or man-made sources (such as coal-burning or other industrial pollution) mercury can be converted by bacteria to a more dangerous form—methylmercury—which accumulates in the fatty tissues of fish. While trace amounts of mercury are present in many types of fish, it becomes most concentrated in large, predatory fish such as swordfish and sharks. Most harmful to the developing brains of unborn children and young children, mercury affects cognitive, motor, and sensory functions.

In 2004 the U.S. Food and Drug Administration (FDA) and the Environmental Protection Agency (EPA) issued new guidelines for limiting exposure to mercury for those most at risk: young children and unborn babies. The guidelines are for women who might become pregnant, women who are pregnant, mothers who are nursing their babies, and those who prepare food for young children. Here are their recommendations for adult consumption:

- Do not eat shark, swordfish, king mackerel, or tilefish because they contain high levels of mercury. Eat up to 12 ounces (two average meals) a week of a variety of fish and shellfish that are lower in mercury. Five of the most commonly eaten fish that are low in mercury are shrimp, canned light tuna, salmon, pollack, and catfish. The Environmental Working Group (EWG) recommends when possible to choose wild and canned Alaskan salmon instead of farmed and to eat farmed salmon no more than once a month. There are studies showing that farm-raised salmon contains higher levels of toxic substances, such as polychlorinated biphenyls (PCBs), than wild salmon.

- Take special care with albacore ("white") tuna, which has more mercury than canned light tuna. If you eat albacore, eat no more than 6 ounces in any week. When you choose 6 ounces of another fish during that week, make sure it is not one that is high in mercury. If you prefer tuna steak to canned tuna, use the same precaution as with albacore. It, too, is high in mercury. Eat no more of it than 6 ounces in a given week.

- Check local advisories about the safety of fish caught by family and friends in your local lakes, rivers, and coastal areas. If no advice is available, eat up to 6 ounces (one average meal) per week of fish you catch from local waters, but don't consume any other fish during that week.

Follow these same recommendations when feeding fish and shellfish to your young child, but serve smaller portions. Although a single serving of fish for an adult is about 6 ounces, it is only about 2 or 3 ounces for a small child. Note that fish sticks and fast-food sandwiches are commonly made from fish that are low in mercury.

For further information about the risks of mercury in fish and shellfish, contact the organizations listed in Appendix E, "Helpful Resources."

Review and Safety Checklist

✓ Choose a clean, well-maintained grocery store when shopping for your family. Check food packaging—whether you're buying baby food or food for the rest of the family—and check it again when you are ready to serve it. Heed sell by and use by dates. Avoid foods whose packaging contains dents, chips, and rust.

✓ Know when and when not to use the microwave to heat your baby's food.

✓ Don't store opened baby food too long; label unused food when you put it in the refrigerator.

✓ Investigate your water supply. If you are on a public water system, read a copy of the latest Consumer Confidence Report. If you are on a private water system, contact the state and local health departments or a cooperative extension agent for recommendations. Take appropriate steps to ensure safe consumption by boiling or filtering tap water, or avoiding it entirely by buying bottled water.

✓ Keep hard, round foods away from your child, and take care with sticky foods. Stay equally vigilant when you take your child to a restaurant.

✓ If you or your spouse has a family history of allergies, consult with your doctor if you are pregnant or nursing and with your child's pediatrician to decrease the risk of your child developing food allergies.

✓ To reduce the risk of food-borne illness, avoid:

✓ soft, unprocessed cheeses

✓ raw, runny, or soft-cooked eggs

✓ raw or undercooked meat, poultry, fish, or shellfish

✓ raw sprouts

✓ and unpasteurized milk, juice, or cider.

✓ Children, women who are planning to become pregnant, and pregnant or nursing women should not eat fish that is high in mercury.

✓ Thoroughly wash fruits and vegetables before using. Toss out damaged produce.

✓ Take care with wild mushrooms and never give honey to a child in the first year of life.

✓ Buy only meat, poultry, or seafood that has been refrigerated or frozen. Place these foods in plastic bags to keep juices from leaking out.

✓ Refrigerate perishables.

✓ When cutting boards, utensils, plates, counters, and hands have been touched by raw meat, poultry, or seafood, wash them thoroughly before they come in contact with cooked food or raw vegetables and fruits.

✓ Wash lids of canned foods and beverages before opening, clean the can opener frequently, and use paper towels to clean kitchen surfaces.

✓ Choose a safe thawing method that suits you and your family, either in the refrigerator, in a sealed bag in cold water, or in the microwave oven.

✓ Always use a food thermometer when you cook.

✓ Before eating, insist on clean hands all around, from baby to the one who serves the food.

Bathroom Safety

In the olden days (that were not so golden), folks had to go outside to use the privy, and the greatest danger—aside from the risk of falling in—was the possibility of running into a skunk or stepping in what the chickens had left behind. Those dangers were rendered obsolete with the advent of the modern, indoor bathroom, and since that time we've come a long, long way. However, even if you have the most luxurious bathroom with the most up-to-date accoutrements, there may be worse dangers there than our great-great grandparents could have imagined.

Never assume your child is too young or has motor skills too poorly developed to get himself into trouble. He may have talents of which you are unaware. You may think your docile child would not have the desire to climb up counters or open cabinets, but he is an explorer, discovering a new world. Take measures to keep your child away from danger.

A hook-and-eye latch high on the outside of the bathroom door will enable you to keep your toddler out of the bathroom, even if you have been distracted for a moment or two. When you have read more of this chapter, you'll better understand why this is a

DO IT YOURSELF!

Making the doorstop safe.

When is a doorstop a hazard? When your child can reach it. The spring action will catch her attention, and she can pull off the plastic tip easily, presenting a choking hazard. There are two solutions:

- Replace the stops near the floor with ones near the top of the door.

- Install solid one-piece doorstops made of polyethylene. These are available in hardware stores and through mail order catalogues.

good idea. On the other hand, a locked door can become a problem if the lock is engaged inside the room—and your toddler is inside alone. (In fact, she may have been the one who locked the door!) If your bedroom or bathroom door has an inside lock, practice opening it from the outside against the day when you'll need to do it in a hurry. Some locks are relatively simple to open with a small screwdriver. You can also remove the door locks, but a less drastic action is to place a towel over the tops of doors to prevent them from closing completely.

Measures to Prevent Burns

Any family member can receive a serious burn from scalding water coming from the faucet of a sink, bathtub or shower. Children are particularly vulnerable because they have thin skin. The risks of severe scalding can occur with temperatures over 120°F. In fact, scalding water kills about 100 people in this country each year. Water at a temperature of 140°F will produce third-degree burns on a child in 3 seconds! A temperature 20 degrees lower gives you about 5 minutes to react before such a burn can occur, and it will still get yourself and your dishes clean.

DO IT YOURSELF!

Prevent scalding.

- Set the thermostat for your water heater at 120°F or lower.

- If you live in an apartment building, check with the property manager to make sure the water heater is set to this temperature.

- Test the water coming out of the tap again, after you have made adjustments.

- Be aware that 120°F water can still burn your little one, so always mix hot water with cold water before it touches your child's skin.

- For additional protection, you can purchase an antiscald device; prices start at about $15. Install it on the tub faucet or other bathroom fixtures. This device shuts off the water before it reaches a temperature that could harm your child.

- You can also buy a thermometer for $3-$5 to make sure the temperature is safe. A comfortable water temperature for the child is near his own body temperature, around 98°F-100°F. Never exceed a water temperature of 100°F.

Stay Out of Too-Hot Water!

The first measure in protecting the family, therefore, is to make sure your water heater is set so it cannot scald your child. (See the sidebar for steps you can take and devices you can buy.)

Be Vigilant Around Hot Water

With or without devices, there are precautions for saving your child from being scalded.

- When filling the bathtub, start with cold water, then add hot. Turn off the hot water first. This way you reduce the likelihood that the water will get too hot or your child will get burned from the hot metal faucet.

- Before letting your child get into the water, move your hand back and forth for several seconds, testing its feel on your skin and making sure there are no hot spots. Before your child enters the tub, be sure the faucet is completely turned off.

- When placing your child in the tub, position her with her back facing the faucet. If she doesn't see the faucet, she won't be tempted to play with it.

- To avoid the danger of your child bumping her head, as well as touching hot metal, you may wish to purchase a foam-rubber protective device that slips over the faucet and handles.

- Bath mats put directly on the floor of the tub should always be used to keep your child from slipping and falling. These can be purchased for about $15.

Around Any Water: Be There!

Carefully and constantly supervise! Regardless of the number of devices you install and the care you take in making sure the temperature is safe, there is no substitute for being there. Always be there! Constant adult supervision is essential when a young child takes a bath or shower.

Never Leave Your Child Alone with Any Water

Never leave, even for a moment, for although the temperature is just right and the baby's bottom is firmly in place on a bath mat, there is still a danger of drowning. I highly recommend that you don't use a bath seat. Parents get a false sense of security from such items and may be tempted to leave the baby unattended for a moment. Dozens of babies have drowned when they fell out of the seat or the seat's suction cups loosened from the tub. Your child must be within arm's reach every second. If the doorbell or phone rings while your child is in the bathtub, either ignore the sound or take your child with you to the phone or door. Immediately empty the water out of the tub or any container after you have used it.

Drowning is the second leading cause of unintentional injury-related death among children ages 1 to 14. The majority of drownings and near-drownings occur in residential swimming pools, hot tubs, and spas. Children under age 1 most often drown in bathtubs, buckets, and toilets. Standing water anywhere poses a drowning hazard. In fact, a small child can drown in as little as 1 inch of water. A toilet, bucket, or pail may be as dangerous as a backyard pool or ocean. Keep small children away from any liquid-filled bucket; particularly hazardous are 5-gallon buckets. Because a child's head is so heavy, he cannot push himself out if he topples into water headfirst. A momentary lapse of adult supervision, even 4 to 6 minutes—the time it takes to answer the phone or door—can cause tragedy. Drowning is a silent death; it is unlikely that a child with his nose and mouth in the water will be able to scream.

Take these precautions: Empty any bucket or container immediately after you have finished using it, and store it out of reach. It's especially important for pails and buckets kept outside to be turned upside down because they can collect rainwater. If you are temporarily interrupted while using a bucket, move it to a safe place. Keep the toilet seat cover closed at all times when it is not in use and install a toilet lock. This device is easy for adults to unlock, but it will keep your child out. Make the bathroom off-limits except for bath and potty times.

Care with Electrical Appliances

Don't you feel better knowing how easy it is to avoid these dangers? Because you exercise caution, bathroom water will neither scald nor drown your baby. Now look around the bathroom. No matter its size, there may be other dangers lurking there.

Remember That Water and Electricity Do Not Mix

Do you have appliances with electric cords in the bathroom? Chances are, you have a hair dryer or curling iron, and possibly an electric razor that must be plugged in. Water and electricity don't mix. If an electrical appliance gets wet when it is plugged in, the user can be electrocuted. Certainly, if such an appliance is dropped into water, the person in the water—especially a child—can be killed.

Have a Professional Install Ground Fault Circuit Interrupters

When purchasing any electrical appliance, look for the mark of a recognized testing lab, such as UL (Underwriters Laboratories) or ETL (Electrical Testing Laboratories). Unless you live in an old home, you probably have GFCIs (ground fault circuit interrupters) installed. Here's the time frame: The National Electrical Code has required GFCIs in outdoor receptacles since 1973, bathroom receptacles since 1975, garage outlets since 1978, and receptacles in crawl spaces and unfinished basements since 1990. If you do not have them installed in those places in your house or you need to take temporary measures, you may purchase portable GFCIs at a hardware store for plugging into electrical outlets. If you do not already have them, you'll do better in the long run to have a qualified electrician install GFCIs in all electrical receptacles inside and outside your home near water sources. (This is not a place to cut corners.) The GFCI automatically shuts off electricity flow when it detects electricity entering a body and grounding the flow. Even with GFCIs in your bathroom, avoid using an electrical appliance there or around other water sources. If the worst happens—perhaps at the home of friends—and an appliance does fall into the water, do not pull it from the water until you are certain it is unplugged. Always keep electrical cords out of the reach of your children.

Always Unplug an Appliance Immediately after You Use It

Even if the switch is off, the appliance is still electrically live if it is plugged in. Since the early 1990s, hair dryers have had built-in shock protection devices to prevent electrocution if they fall into water. Buy a new dryer with a large, rectangular plug. Store such appliances safely out of the reach of your child, preferably outside the bathroom. Never place or store any appliance where it can fall or be pulled into the bath or sink, and watch out for the cords! A dangling cord is a mighty temptation to a child. An appliance falling on his head may not electrocute him, but he can certainly be injured by it.

Don't Leave a Hot Appliance Unattended

All the approval ratings and safety devices in the world won't keep that appliance from getting hot. Don't forget that it will stay hot for at least 5 minutes after being turned off. To avoid skin burns, put it down on a stable surface so that it won't fall, and don't leave it unattended while it's still hot. Store it after it has cooled. One appliance designed to be hot is a bathroom heater, but don't use it without a guard around the heating element. Even with the guard, do not leave a functioning heater and a child alone together in a room.

Poisons in the Cabinet

We've taken steps to protect the child from being scalded, drowned, and electrocuted, but there is one more grave danger in this necessary room. Think about it. What do you keep in the cabinet under the sink or in the so-called medicine cabinet?

Find the Poison and Take It Out

Now is the time to move poisonous products you kept safely in the bathroom before you had a child. These include rubbing alcohol, mouthwash, prescription medicine, iron supplements, and over-the-counter medicine such as pain relievers. Any of those products can be mistaken by the child for something he has been allowed to have. (See Chapter 10, "Common Poisons in the Home.") Securely lock poisonous and hazardous products (such as razors, tweezers, and scissors) out of the sight and reach of children.

DO IT YOURSELF!

Practice safety with medicine.

- Never call medicine candy, even if you are trying to get the child to take the medicine.

- If you have a chronic disorder and take medicine on a regular basis, don't take your medicine in front of your child; she'll try to imitate you.

- Don't let her play with medicine bottles.

- Never give medication in the dark. You may pick up the wrong medicine or give an inaccurate dosage.

- Keep all your medications in child-resistant packaging, but remember that these lids are child-resistant, not childproof. They buy you only some extra seconds.

- Securely close caps after using a medication and promptly return the item to its place after using it.

- Discard all expired and unlabeled medicines by flushing them down the toilet, then rinsing the containers thoroughly before discarding.

- Don't put pills in your handbag where a child can easily get them. Consider anyone else's bag as you would a loaded gun. You don't know what's in there!

Review and Safety Checklist

   ✓ Protect your child from scalding in the tub or at the sink by:

      ✓ Adjusting your home water heater thermostat to 120°F or lower

      ✓ Purchasing and installing an antiscald device

      ✓ Turning on cold water first, then adding hot, when filling the bath tub; turn off the hot water first

      ✓ Feeling the water for hot spots and mixing it around before the child gets into the tub

      ✓ Using a thermometer to see that the water temperature is 98°F to100°F.

✓ Protect your child from being electrocuted or burned by:

   ✓ Having ground fault circuit interrupters installed in the bathroom and anywhere a receptacle and a water source are present

   ✓ Making sure your appliances have the UL or ETL mark of approval

   ✓ Keeping electrical appliances away from sinks and tubs, unplugging appliances after use, and tying up electrical cords so they don't dangle

   ✓ Putting hot appliances on a stable surface after using, away from small hands

   ✓ Carefully supervising the use of any appliance that gets hot and promptly putting it away after it cools

✓ Protect your child from drowning by:

   ✓ Staying with your child every second he is in the bathroom, especially in the tub

   ✓ Installing locks on the toilet and always keeping the lid closed

   ✓ Immediately emptying the water from the tub, sink, or any container after it has been used

   ✓ Keeping your child away from any liquid-filled bucket or container

✓ Protect your child from poisoning by:

   ✓ Locking up poisons that are commonly kept in the bathroom

   ✓ Securely closing the child-resistant cap after using a medication and promptly returning the item to its proper place

Part II

Safety Measures for Every Living Space

Before a child came to live in your home, you could afford to be careless about where you put things. Your only problem then was whether you'd be able to find your handbag or your keys, or an earring or watch. It's best to start creating new habits for yourself early, even before your baby is born. Once she arrives, you'll have plenty to do.

Not only will you want to change the pattern of tossing small items on a convenient chair, low table, or shelf, but you will also—before your baby begins to crawl—want to get into the habit of regularly and carefully inspecting your home for small objects. Crawling around every room is one way to do it if your knees will take the pain. Look under beds, furniture, and cushions, and in bags and pockets that a child might be able to reach.

To understand what you're looking for, go back to the axiom from Chapter 1: Children put everything in their mouths. Look for anything that is small enough to fit: coins, small batteries, small balls, marbles, crayon pieces, keys, jewelry, paper clips, buttons, pop-can tops, plastic bags, wrappers, nails, tacks, screws, safety pins, and removable rubber tips on doorstops.

Also look for items on your child's clothing that might come off. Use Velcro instead of buttons and avoid jeweled decorations that the child can pull off. If your baby's clothes or toys have plastic labels or decals, remove and properly discard them before he pulls them off himself . . . and puts them in his mouth.

With that introduction to "all-through-the-house" caution, let's move to some specific hazards in the home. In Chapter 5 you'll learn how to prevent two kinds of fall-related injuries: first, the child's falling from stairs, windows, or furniture, and second, heavy items that can fall on the child. Chapter 6 takes us to areas outside the house, as well as the garage, workshop, and basement. For the backyard, we will discuss safety guidelines for pools and around the playground and barbecue grill. Safety with pets is the topic in Chapter 7. We detail fire safety in Chapter 8 and gun safety in Chapter 9.

> **DO IT YOURSELF!**
>
> *What to do with plastic bags . . .*
>
> - Tie plastic bags and wraps in knots and discard, or store them locked away from children.
>
> - Don't forget to remove all dry-cleaning bags from your closets. A child can suffocate when a plastic bag covers his face.

Dangers surrounding common poisons we keep at home are considered in Chapter 10, and Chapter 11 provides guidelines concerning environmental hazards that can affect the entire family but especially babies.

Special problem areas that are part of having an office at home are explained in Chapter 12, with a note about knowing your own limitations. Even if your office is at home, there will still be times when you'll need to hire a sitter or find a reputable day care center. You'll learn how to do it wisely in Chapter 13. To finish the section, Chapter 14 lists items that should be part of your first aid and disaster supplies kits. A form to use for emergency numbers completes the chapter.

Preventing Falls in the Home

F alls are a leading cause of hospitalization and emergency room visits for children. Someone might joke that we need not worry about small children falling because they don't have as far to fall, but every conscientious parent knows infants and toddlers are more vulnerable to serious injuries caused by falls. If you must leave your baby alone for a moment, make sure she is in a safe place, such as a crib. If she is on a changing table, a bed, or any furniture from which she can roll over and fall off, do not leave her for a second.

The greater risk for infants is associated with falls on stairs, from furniture, and in baby walkers. For toddlers, falls from windows present the greater risk. On the other side of the coin is the danger of being a victim of something falling. In addition to discussing things that are not designed to fall but do, I'll consider a product that is supposed to fall: the garage door. The issue is not to keep the door from falling, but to make sure there is nothing or no one under it when it comes down. Just in case, an auto-reverse device equipped with an entrapment protection feature is crucial.

Stairs

Keep Stairways Lit and Clear of Clutter

One of the simplest ways to make stairs safe is to light them. This helps everyone in the family, but it is especially important if you have a baby in your arms. Have a light switch at both the bottom and the top of the stairs. Keep night-lights at each end, as well, in case of power failure.

In fact, no part of the house should be dark when your family is moving about. Power-failure night-lights are like regular night-lights except that they automatically switch on as emergency lights any time the power fails. Prices start at around $10 each. In addition to placing them at each end of the stairs, put them in halls, bedrooms, and bathrooms, too, so that the entire family will always have a lighted path.

Night-lights at floor level, especially those that look like toys, may attract your crawling baby to the socket. If possible, install a night-light in a socket out of the baby's reach. Use night lights with child-safety features; look for ones that completely enclose the bulbs and have safety tabs that hinder a child's ability to remove it from an outlet.

Even when stairs are well lit, anyone can trip on objects left there. Stairs and landings should be kept free of any clutter. If you are in the habit of placing items on the stairs to be picked up the next time you go up or down, break the habit. And don't allow toys, boxes, or books to be placed there at any time of the day. Steps are not storage units. Another tip: Don't wax the stairs or the landing area.

Purchase and Install Safety Gates, and Know When to Take Them Down

When your baby begins to move—even before he can crawl—install safety gates at the top and bottom of stairs, carefully following the manufacturer's instructions. A pressure gate, which attaches to the walls with pressure rather than with screws, is okay at the bottom of the stairs, but never put a pressure gate at the top. Such a gate can give way if a child leans on it. If you use a pressure-bar gate at the bottom, install it with the bar side away from the baby so the bar cannot be used as a toehold for climbing over.

When your child is old enough to climb over a gate (when she is about 2 years of age), remove it. When it comes down to it, a gate should be difficult to climb over, no matter what the child's age. Choose gates with vertical slats rather than horizontal ones, and make sure the slats are no more than 2 3/8 inches apart. Even better, choose a gate made from fine mesh or Plexiglas. Never use accordion-style baby gates manufactured prior to February 1985; an entrapment and strangulation hazard exists. These gates have

V-shaped openings along the top edge and diamond-shaped openings between the slats that are large enough to entrap a child's head.

No matter what materials are in the gate or how it is attached, do not rely on the gate (or any other baby equipment) to keep your precious one safe. A gate should never be used in place of close adult supervision. Once your child is moving around on her own, with or without gates, the size of the space between stair railings is important. The space should never be more than 3 1/2 inches wide. (See the sidebar under the section in this chapter titled "Balconies, Decks, and Porches.")

Teach Safe Walking

Practice walking up and down the stairs with your toddler. Teach him that he should always hold on to the hand railing when going up or down. (Be sure there is a sturdy railing on both sides that your child can reach.) Don't be shy about inventing solutions of your own. When my children were first starting to climb steps, I positioned the bottom gate on the third or fourth carpeted step to allow them some supervised climbing experience on the bottom few stairs. That way a fall would not be from a great height. No matter what kind of surface—rugs, tile, or wood—is in your home, don't allow children to play on the stairs.

Keep in mind that children (and adults, too!) can easily slip on scatter rugs. If possible, to prevent tumbles, remove the rugs or secure them with double-faced adhesive carpet tape or nonskid matting under each rug.

Furniture

Look around your home. Nearly every item can either fall or be fallen from. The possibility of falling furniture may be a novel idea to you if you're new at this parent-of-a-toddler business, but there are a variety of ways furniture can tip. Your tiny beloved may fall against the furniture, causing it to tilt, or he may climb up on it, perhaps in an innocent effort to retrieve something he wants. Down will come baby, bookcase and all! Maybe he'll try to move the furniture, or perhaps he simply wants to sit on it. It's possible that he's just trying to be helpful by opening or closing a door, drawer, or compartment. If it's moveable, it can fall.

If you're used to making your own improvements around your home, you can probably figure out some of the precautions you should take to keep furniture from falling. To enable you to cover all the bases, I have a few hints.

Avoid Buying Certain Items

Don't purchase furniture pieces with wide shelves or footholds, which can encourage climbing. Avoid freestanding items, such as floor lamps and standing coat racks (which are sometimes as free-falling as they are freestanding).

Anchor Large and Heavy Furnishings Securely to the Wall

Heavy items such as bookshelves, heavy appliances (including the kitchen oven), and entertainment centers can tip even when they are set against a wall. Use angle braces or anchors to secure such furniture and objects to the wall. Use the same preventive measures for cabinets, dressers, chests, and bureaus, too, but with furniture like this, you must go one step further. If it has drawers, install safety latches designed to keep children from opening them. Even if your chest or bureau is secured to the wall, a child climbing on the drawers could slip and suffer a deadly fall.

Arrange Furniture with Safety in Mind

Items such as the TV and stereo system should be placed on sturdy, low furniture and set as far back toward the wall as possible. For these items, too, you may wish to use wall mounts. Table lamps are safer at the back of a table, close to the wall. For lighting rooms where a toddler roams, a ceiling light fixture or wall lamp is best. To keep the center of gravity low, place heavy items on lower shelves. Anything heavy and able to be tipped should be stored in an inaccessible place. In fact, any knickknacks or breakable items should be kept out of your toddler's reach, right along with the heavy stuff. Avoid using pedestal tables to hold weighty items.

Another hazard associated with the TV set is the VCR or DVD player. To keep small fingers (as well as grilled cheese sandwiches) out of the front-loading VCR or DVD, keep it out of the child's reach or attach a lock.

Use Furniture Padding

Not even a safety advocate like me would tell you to store or get rid of all your furniture, but it is an inescapable fact that every small child bumps into household furniture. Keep the furniture, but cover the corners! You can cushion the bumps and falls by attaching corner and edge protectors to all sharp edges on chairs, bookshelves, cabinets, fireplace hearths, and all table and countertops—including that fixture of American living rooms, the coffee table. My husband and I, when our children were toddlers, did something you might consider: we put the coffee table in storage for the first 4 years of our child's life. That can seem like a long time, especially if you have more than one child, but we took that step after our son used the coffee table as a launching pad. He found out he couldn't fly, and we decided we could do without the table.

Windows

Prevent Your Child's Access to Windows

I covered this point in Chapter 1, "Creating a Safe Nursery." To reiterate: Do not keep cribs, chairs, benches, tables, toy boxes, or even a bookcase near the window. Such items are an open invitation for the child to climb up to the window.

Install Window Guards—Don't Depend on Screens

Yes, you've arranged the furniture with safety in mind, but a toddler can get places you never dreamed he could. Don't depend on screens. These are no more than flimsy barriers to keep bugs out. If possible, when you open a window, open it from the top, not the bottom. Avoid a false sense of security; a child can fall from a window that is opened more than 4 inches. Keep your windows closed and locked when children are present.

A child can be severely injured or die from falling from even a first-floor window, so for the best protection against falls from windows, install window guards on every window in your home. For windows on the sixth floor and below, install window guards that adults and older children can easily open in case of fire. For the seventh floor and above, permanent window guards should be used. Before you make a purchase or install guards, check local building and fire codes.

Window guards adjust for width, but they are sized differently for different window heights. Measure your windows carefully. The guards should screw into the side of the window frame and have bars no more than 4 inches apart. In June 2000, ASTM (American Society for Testing and Materials) established voluntary safety standards for window guards. These standards ensure that window guards designed for single-family homes or the lower floors of apartment buildings are strong enough to prevent falls and have simple emergency release mechanisms for use in the event of a fire. Be sure your guards meet this standard. Window guards are available from a variety of suppliers throughout the country. Visit www.windowguard.org to find a local retailer in your area.

A less costly option is to use a window-stopping device. The device attaches to the inside of the window frame to prevent the window from opening more than 4 inches. These can be found at most hardware stores and are easy to install. Some new windows have window stops already installed. Reinforce with your children the rule that they are not to lean out of or play near open windows.

Another type of window is the sliding glass door. Herein lies another kind of danger. While your child isn't likely to fall out of it, she can certainly collide with it. To prevent her from crashing into a glass door, thinking it is open, apply large, colorful safety stickers at the child's eye-level. To keep your child safely inside, use a door lock made for sliding glass doors and secure the doors with a bar in the door track. Don't let your children play around sliding glass doors.

Balconies, Decks, and Porches

Keep small children away from balconies, decks, and porches by keeping all access doors locked. Install child-resistant locks on the

---

DO IT YOURSELF!

Install proper railings.

- Railings should have a minimum height of 42 inches.

- Spaces between the railing and slats should be no wider than 3 ½ inches.

- Install a railing guard made of Plexiglas, plastic, or mesh if spaces are too wide apart. (For outdoor use, make sure materials are designed to withstand the elements, including UV.) Never use safety netting or any railing guard on railings that are spaced too far apart to provide adequate support for the product. If such is the case, remodeling is necessary.

backyard door. Make sure any children playing in these areas are closely supervised.

Take steps to safeguard children near railings

Even if you are carefully supervising your child, safety measures must always be in place. Do not leave plants, planters, chairs, benches, or any other object that a child could climb up on anywhere near the railing. Be aware that ambitious children may try to move a chair over to the railing to "get a better look." Ensure they cannot do this with deterrent means appropriate to the object.

Make sure proper railings are in place (see sidebar) and maintain them regularly. Do not allow them to become loose. Never leave your child unattended and do not rely on any safety item to keep your child safe.

Garage Door

Because the garage door is the largest moving object in your home, it needs special consideration. A child can suffer permanent brain damage—or die—as a result of an incident involving an automatic door opener.

Not an Option: Install Safety Devices on Your Automatic Door

As of 1982, automatic garage-door openers are required to have an auto-reverse mechanism to reverse the door's direction if it comes in contact with an object. If you have an older opener without an automatic reversal system, it should be replaced immediately. When purchasing a new garage-door opener, make sure it carries the mark of a recognized testing lab such as UL (Underwriters Laboratories) or ETL (Electrical Testing Laboratories).

For further protection, federal law has required that automatic garage-door openers manufactured on or after January 1, 1993, be equipped with an additional entrapment protection feature, such as a photoelectric sensor. This electric eye projects an invisible light beam across the inside of the garage door opening. If anything interrupts the beam while the door is going down, it will automatically reverse the door before making contact. If you don't wish to tackle this project yourself, a company that installs garage-door openers can install these safety devices.

Refer to the manufacturer's instructions for ongoing maintenance of the garage door and operator as well as regular testing of
the safety reversing features. Inspect your garage door monthly to
see if it is operating properly. If it is not, disconnect the automatic
opener from the door (as specified in the owner's manual) and
manually open and close the door until it is repaired.

Additional precautions include placing all activation buttons at
least 6 feet above the floor, out of the hands of your child. Also,
keep the remote control for the door locked in the glove compartment of your car. Do not let it seem to be a toy; do not let a child
operate or play with the opener.

Don't Take Anything for Granted

Safety devices can fail. Make sure you have a full view of the
garage door when you are using the opener. Always check for
obstructions—especially live ones such as children and pets. Keep
them a safe distance away from the door while it is moving and
continue to watch the door until it has completely opened or completely closed. Don't pull out of the driveway until the door has
completely shut.

No one should be allowed to run underneath a moving door.
That goes for you, too, Mom and Dad! Be role models. Warn your
child of the potential dangers of crossing under a moving garage
door. Store children's play items away from the garage door, thus
removing the temptation to run under a moving door to retrieve
something.

Juvenile Equipment

Being careful when you make a purchase is the first step in preventing injuries with baby equipment. Look for the JPMA (Juvenile
Products Manufacturer Association) certification label. And when
using baby equipment, always follow the manufacturer's instructions on assembly, care, and use. However, there is one piece of
equipment we see all the time that is simply not a good choice.

Don't Buy a Wheeled Baby Walker

Each year, an average of 2 children die as a result of baby-walker-related injuries. In 2002, nearly 4,600 children ages 4 and under
were treated in hospital emergency rooms for baby-walker-related
injuries. Most of these injuries—and the most severe—are caused

when a child falls down stairs with the walker. Even when there are no stairs or when the safety gates are always locked, your child can still tip it over, fall out of it, or reach places where he can pull hot foods or heavy objects down on himself. You don't have to take my word for it. Both the National SAFE KIDS Campaign and the American Academy of Pediatrics recommend that you not use a wheeled baby walker at all. Using a stationary activity center is still fun for your baby, and it is a much safer choice.

Maintain Specific Standards If You Choose a Baby Walker Anyway

If you choose to use a wheeled baby walker, the Consumer Products Safety Commission (CPSC) strongly recommends that you replace (and destroy) a walker made before 1997 with a new one. Newer walkers meet new standards and are certified by the JPMA. To meet the certification, the baby walker must be too wide to fit through a standard doorway or have features—such as a gripping mechanism—to stop the walker at the edge of a step.

Use the walker only on smooth surfaces. It can tip over when it encounters the edge of a carpet or throw rug; a raised threshold can be treacherous, too. Even on a smooth surface with no impediments, your child is not safe on her own when she is in the walker. Don't neglect supervision—keep your baby in full view while she uses the walker. This piece of equipment is not a babysitter. One second of your inattention can result in an injury. Because the walker enables your child to get more places more quickly, putting more items within her reach, all the previous words of caution take on new significance.

Whatever you choose to use, a walker or stationary activity center, use it only for brief periods. Your baby needs the exercise of crawling to develop coordination and strength in her arms and legs.

Stay Vigilant When Using a Changing Table

Buy or build a changing table that has high sides and is sturdy and stable. Safety straps are a must. When using the table, always use those safety straps. Even with them, never leave your child unattended, not even for a second. You won't need to leave that squirming little bundle of joy, even for an instant, if you keep diapers and toiletries within your reach. Be sure they are not within your baby's reach, however. Most of those items present a danger if they go into the baby's mouth, and you know where she likes to put things. If she gets her hands on them and doesn't put them in her mouth, she is likely to pitch them, just to make you go fetch. That's a fun game when she's not in danger of falling off a table.

Use a High Chair with a Wide Base, Locks, and Safety Straps

Select a high chair with a wide, stable base. It should have a crotch post, a waist strap, and a crotch strap that are independent of the tray. Test the straps before you buy, choosing ones that are sturdy as well as easy to fasten and unfasten. If they're difficult to fasten, you'll be tempted not to use them from time to time.

If you have chosen a folding high chair, make sure it is locked each time you set it up. When you use any high chair, make sure the tray is locked securely in place, but don't rely on it to keep the child from falling out. Your child can also slide down beneath the tray and strangle. Always use the crotch strap and the belt around the waist.

You know the drill by now: Place the chair far away from any table, counter, or wall so your little darling can't use them to push off. Don't allow him to stand on the chair. Stay close.

Use a Stroller That Will Not Tip and Has Convenient Brakes

A stroller should have a base wide enough to prevent it from tipping over, even when your baby leans over to one side. It should have a strong, durable safety belt that is easy to open and close. If the seat adjusts to a reclining position, make sure the stroller won't tip over backward when the child lies down. If there is a shopping basket for carrying items attached to the stroller, the basket should be low on the back of the stroller or directly over the rear of the wheels.

Anything with wheels should have brakes. Stroller brakes should actually lock the wheels and be convenient to operate. Having brakes on two sides provides an extra measure of safety.

Follow Guidelines for Safe Stroller Use

Perhaps the premier safety rule for use of the stroller is never to leave a child unattended. In addition, other children should not be allowed to push it or get into it when the baby is in it. It's probably a good idea just to never let children play with the stroller, even without the baby's presence. The following tips help ensure safe stroller use:

- Before you put the baby in a stroller, use its locking device to prevent unintentional folding.

- Apply the brakes to limit rotation of the wheels when the stroller is stationary—this means when you are putting the baby in or taking her out, or parking it for some reason.

- Secure the safety belts, always!

- Close the leg openings. When used in a carriage position, if the openings are not closed at the crotch, a baby can slip through feet first and become entrapped by his head between the seat and the hand-rest bar. Strangulation could result.

- Don't hang your handbag, diaper bag, or other items over the handles. This can cause even a stable stroller to tip.

- When you fold or unfold the stroller, or when the seat back is being reclined, keep your child away from areas that may pinch him.

Check Your Playpen/Play Yard for Dangerous Design Flaws

In the past decade, millions of North American playpens—many of them popular brand-name models—were designed with dangerous flaws. In some cases, children died when the top rails collapsed and entrapped their necks. These playpens had a hinge in the center of each top rail that had to be rotated to set up the playpen; if the hinge was not rotated completely, the top rail could collapse and form a V. Playpens made since 1997 have top rails that automatically snap into place and do not need to be rotated when you set up the playpen.

Another hazard is protruding rivets. Some toddlers strangled when loose clothing or pacifier strings tied around their neck got caught on the rivets. (Remember, nothing should be tied around a child's neck.)

If you own a playpen, check with the manufacturer or contact the CPSC to find out if yours is safe. In the recalls section below there is a discussion about ways to learn about recalls. Even if your playpen is fairly new, be sure to check.

Use Your Playpen Correctly

A playpen with a safe design but used inappropriately can harm your child. (Please refer to the safety guidelines outlined in Chapter 1, "Creating a Safe Nursery.") Three more precautions are noted below:

- Never leave your baby in a mesh playpen with the drop-side down. Babies can suffocate if they roll into the gap between the mattress and the loose mesh side.

- Pay attention to the pad. Use only the mattress pad that comes with the playpen. The mattress pad should fit tightly against all four sides. Don't add an extra mattress. Babies can get trapped between the mattress and sides.

- Give it up when the time comes. Do not place a child in a playpen once she has reached 35 inches in height—about the age of 2—or has become persistent in her efforts to climb out.

Recall Information

Even when you have used the greatest care and looked for appropriate labels, there can still be a product recall. That's one of the reasons you'll want to fill out the registration form. If there is one available for that product, send it to the manufacturer. Only if you are registered can the company notify you of a recall.

Recalls can occur at any stage of a product's life cycle, so you must stay up-to-date regarding everything you use. It is now easier than ever to be informed about recalls. Six federal agencies have gotten together to form a website: www.recalls.gov. At this link, you can see the latest recalls in consumer products, motor vehicles, boats, food, medicine, cosmetics, and environmental products. Just click on the desired topic.

This is one-stop shopping at its best. For example, if you have purchased a playpen, you can sign up at the new site for CPSC recall notices. Of course, you may go to the individual agency websites, too. Those agencies and their websites, along with other ways to contact the agencies, can be found in Appendix D, "Recall Information."

When Bedtime Means a Real Bed

Regardless of construction, a bed is not a safe sleeping or napping area for an infant or any child under 2 years of age.

When Your Toddler Is Ready to Use a Bed, Know the Rules

Put the mattress on the floor or as close to the floor as possible. You may wish to consider installing soft flooring—a thick pad or a gym mat—around the bed to lessen the severity of a fall-related injury. Strictly enforce a policy of no playing or jumping on beds.

Portable bed rails are intended for use on adult beds to help prevent children from falling out of bed. They are not intended for use by children under 2 years of age. If you choose to use portable bed rails, make sure to carefully follow the manufacturer's instructions on assembly, care, and use. Make sure to use two bed rails, one for each side of the bed, even if one side is against the wall. Children can become entrapped and die when they get caught between the bed and wall. The CPSC is presently developing a mandatory safety standard for portable bed rails to require that they not present entrapment and strangulation hazards to young children. Contact the CPSC (800) 638-2772 for more information.

To prevent entrapment with bunk beds, all spaces between the guardrail and the bed frame and in the head- and footboards should be less than 3 1/2 inches and there should be guardrails on both sides. As of July 2000, all bunk beds manufactured or imported for sale in the U.S. must meet these requirements. Children under the age of 6 should never sleep on the top bed.

Review and Safety Checklist

✓ Use power-failure night-lights at the top and bottom of stairs and throughout your home, particularly in halls, bedrooms, and bathrooms.

✓ Install safety gates at the top and bottom of stairs and across open doorways. Do not use a pressure-bar gate at the top of the stairs and keep all gates locked.

✓ Arrange furniture in a way that reduces the risk of tipping. Store heavy or breakable items away from little hands.

✓ Anchor large and heavy furniture and objects securely to the wall, and attach cushioned corner- and edge-protectors on furniture.

✓ Install window guards on every window in your home. Use quick-release mechanisms on any windows that are part of your fire-escape plans. Check local building and fire codes.

✓ Install safety devices on your automatic garage door and always watch it to make sure it completely shuts.

✓ Don't put your baby in a wheeled baby walker.

✓ Use all safety features, such as safety straps, with all baby equipment, such as the changing table, the high chair, and the stroller.

✓ Stay up to date with recall information.

Safety in the Backyard

If your child can't be safe in her own backyard, where can she be safe? You'll be as excited as her when she begins to explore the world outside the four walls of your home. She'll learn what fun she can have, just by smelling flowers, hearing birds, seeing butterflies, touching grass, feeling the breeze as it moves her hair in tempo with the branches of trees overhead. She'll also learn about outdoor activities, and it's up to you to make sure those activities do not hurt her.

First make sure your yard itself is safe by fencing it in. If only the backyard is fenced, never allow your child to play in the front yard. Even if you are right there—and you should always be right there, closely supervising your child!—you may not be able to stop a toddler from darting out into the street.

It follows, of course, that children should never play in the driveway. Even when a car is moving slowly, a child that is hit can be seriously hurt or killed. Toddlers can move quickly, have no sense of danger, and may be out of a driver's line of vision simply because of their short stature.

If there are any poisonous plants in your yard, pull them out. (See Chapter 10, "Common Poisons in the Home," and Appendix B, "Common Poisonous Plants.") No matter how beautiful they are, if they can harm your child, you do not want them. You must also take care concerning the pesticides used in your yard. (See Chapter 11, "Environmental Hazards," under the topic "Pesticides," where you'll find safer methods to eliminate pests.)

Yard work is important for safety, no matter what the season. Repair cracks or chips in cement sidewalks and stairs, and keep those stairs and walkways clear of snow, wet leaves, and other debris.

Before we step into the backyard, we'll consider safety in some spaces that are not outside, but which are not usually considered part of your living space: the garage, the workshop, and the basement. This entire chapter is a do-it-yourself project, so get ready for some down-to-earth (and down-to-water) advice.

Garage, Workshop, and Basement

The garage, workshop, and basement are difficult to make safe even for older children, so keep these rooms strictly off-limits to your young child. High dead bolts or flip locks should be in use to prevent the child's entry into these rooms. Even with those locks in place, you must take safety precautions, just in case your child wanders in (perhaps following you).

Start by first inspecting the room and determining what you really want or need to save. Unnecessary items that are not useful should be discarded. It's a good idea to buy only what you will need for each particular project at hand. The savings for quantity is usually not worth buying a special locked cabinet in which to store the extra material safely. For those items you must keep, get a locking storage cabinet.

Use and Store All Tools Safely

Designate specific places for tools and hang them out of reach of children. Having a place for each tool has the added benefit of prompting all the adults with access to the room to return each tool to its proper place after its use. That makes it a snap to find it the next time you want to use it. Wherever you store your power tools, disconnect them when they are not in use.

Take Extra Precautions When Using and Storing Flammable Liquids

All flammable liquids such as gasoline, paint thinners, and kerosene should be kept in properly labeled, tightly closed, safety-approved containers. These products should be stored out of the reach of children, outside the house in a locked shed or detached garage. Keep them in a well-ventilated place away from any source of ignition, and always take the containers outside to fuel power mowers and other equipment. They produce invisible explosive vapors that can be ignited by a small spark at considerable distances from a flammable substance.

Store All Buckets Upside Down

Remember that a small child can drown in as little as 1 inch of water.

Store and Lock Poisonous Products Out of the Reach of Children

All poisons should have child-resistant caps. Keep all products in their original containers and never mix products. Common items you need to lock away, out of the sight and reach of children, are:

- pest-control products

- weed killers and fertilizers

- car-care products such as antifreeze, motor oil, and windshield-washer solution

- turpentine, paints, and paint thinner

- pool supplies

- kerosene

- art and hobby supplies

- glues and adhesives

- and charcoal lighters.

Install Safety Devices

Your automatic garage door should have an auto-reverse device equipped with an additional entrapment protection feature, such as a photoelectric sensor. Install a smoke alarm in the basement. (Alarms should be installed on every level of the home.) However, NFPA recommends that you do not install smoke alarms in garages or other areas where temperatures could fall below 40°F or exceed 100°F. A carbon monoxide alarm should be installed at least 15 feet from a fuel burning appliance. Carefully follow the manufacturer's installation instructions. As in the rest of the house, you should make sure that alarms are working properly and are properly maintained.

Alarms are further considered in other chapters. Please see Chapter 8 regarding smoke alarms and Chapter 11 for a discussion about carbon monoxide. For more information regarding automatic garage openers, please see Chapter 5.

Control Tripping Hazards

Keep the area clean, particularly the floor. To keep children from tripping against the edge of a ladder and having it fall on them, store the ladder lengthwise (parallel to the floor) rather than leaning against the wall.

Take Precautions to Prevent Entrapment

Entrapment hazards include:

- clothes dryers

- old style latch-type refrigerators

- latch-type freezers

- combination washer-dryer units

- camper ice boxes

- picnic coolers

- and storage chests.

Suffocation deaths occur in such places when children crawl inside and cannot escape. The tight-fitting gasket on most appliances cuts off air to the child, and the insulated construction of the appliances prevents anyone from hearing her cry for help.

Childproof old refrigerators and other appliances that are in storage or are to be discarded. The surest method is to take off the door and leave in the shelves. Keep children away from any currently used item that may present an entrapment hazard by locking the door to the area where it is kept. To keep children from entrapment in your car, make certain it stays locked and the windows are always up.

Keep Your Child Away from Outdoor Power Equipment

Okay, we're almost ready to go outside, but if anyone is using power equipment out there, keep your child indoors and supervised closely at all times. Turn off any power equipment when a child enters a work area. After any outdoor task is complete, store garden tools and other equipment locked out of your child's reach. This goes for mowers and garden tractors, as well as carts or trailers that are pulled behind them. Don't let any child play near a mower, even when it is stationary. Naturally, this proscription is even more important when the mower or tractor is engaged. Such equipment is not a toy; don't let the kids ride on it.

The Outdoors

It is possible that until your child has his first outdoor outing, he has never been bitten or stung by a bug. Another new experience is his exposure to the sun, making him at risk for sunburn. You are certainly in no hurry for him to have any of these experiences. If the weather permits, the best way to protect your child from the sun, bug bites, and ticks is to cover his skin with a hat; a lightweight, long-sleeved shirt; and long pants. Tuck clothing into pants and pant cuffs into socks.

Know What to Do About Ticks

Most tick bites occur during the spring and summer months. Although May through August are high-risk months, ticks are active and can bite any time the temperature is higher than 40°F. Ticks live in woods and tall grass, so to discourage ticks from inhabiting your yard, it is important to keep grass cut short and to remove unwanted vegetation around your home. Don't let children brush up against bushes, trees, leaf litter, or shrubs.

Wear light-colored clothing with a tight weave so that you can spot ticks more easily and prevent contact with the skin. Scan clothes and any exposed skin frequently for ticks while you are outside. After every outing when the temperature has exceeded 40°F, immediately put your child's clothing in the dryer on high heat for about 30 minutes to kill any ticks that might be on them. If clothes have been washed or are damp, an hour may be necessary. Another possibility is to hang the clothes outside, away from the house and oft-traveled paths for several hours. The ticks will drop off.

Bathe your children and perform a head-to-toe tick inspection. Because ticks often attach to the more-hidden hair areas, check especially the groin, armpits, and scalp. It's best to use a magnifying glass, because some ticks are very small, about the size of a poppy seed.

Remember to check all family members, including your pets. (You can be bitten in your home if a pet brings a tick inside.) Contact your local or state health department for more information about ticks and for guidelines concerning the risks of Lyme disease and other tick-borne infections in your geographical area.

Prevent Bug Bites

Teach your child to move slowly and carefully around insects, and dress him in white, beige, or khaki-colored clothing. Bright colors and flowered or floral prints (and scented soaps, lotions, perfumes, or hair sprays) attract bees and other insects. Food aromas attract insects, so don't feed your children outdoors. Other odors

---

DO IT YOURSELF!

Remove ticks.

The American Lyme Disease Foundation has these recommendations:
- Stay calm and don't panic! There is little risk of infection within the first 36-48 hours. The sooner you remove the tick, the better.

- Use a pair of fine-tipped tweezers and place them parallel to the skin.

- Grab the tick as close to the skin as possible (by its head or mouth parts) and pull out gently but firmly.

- Do not grab the tick by its body. The tick is like a balloon full of water; if you grab its body, whatever is in it will be squirted into you! The less agitation, the better.

- Don't use a match, nail polish remover, or petroleum jelly to remove a tick.

- Once you remove the tick, clean the bite with antiseptic and wash your hands with soap and water. Kill the tick by dropping it in alcohol. You may wish to put the tick in a plastic, reclosable bag, and save it so it is available as a reference if infection symptoms start.

- Be aware of early-infection symptoms of Lyme disease. Within days to weeks following a tick bite, 80% of patients will have a red, slowly expanding bull's eye rash (called Erythema Migrans), accompanied by general tiredness, fever, headache, swollen glands, chills, stiff neck, muscle aches, and joint pain.

attract insects, too, so keep your child away from garbage cans and out of gardens when flowers are in bloom. Do not permit children to go barefoot outside. Eliminate breeding places for mosquitoes by getting rid of stagnant water around your home. Mosquitoes prefer to feed from dusk to dawn, so you may want to avoid outdoor activities during that period.

For more information about avoiding bugs that sting and bite, and to learn about mosquito-borne diseases such as West Nile virus, contact your local or state health department.

Use Extreme Caution with Repellents

DEET (chemical name N,N-diethyl-meta-toluamide) is the active ingredient in many insect repellents. It is used to repel biting pests such as mosquitoes and ticks. In areas where insect-borne disease is widespread, it may be necessary to use an effective insect repellent to keep your child safe.

DEET should not be used at all on babies younger than 2 months. Consult your pediatrician for specific recommendations before using DEET on your child. Insect repellents containing DEET should be used sparingly on children and only at the lowest effective concentration appropriate for the amount of time the child will be outdoors. Generally, less than 10% DEET is recommended for use on children. Follow label instructions carefully. In rare cases, some children have experienced adverse effects after application of DEET. Most of the cases of toxicity in children were associated with the use of 10-50% DEET and were related to overdose and misuse. Use as little as you need for your situation and avoid repeat applications. Use only in well-ventilated spaces and do not use near food.

It is best to have children wear lightweight, long-sleeved shirts and long pants, when possible. To reduce exposure to DEET, apply repellent to the clothing—I would put it on the clothes before dressing them—rather than to the skin. Never use it under clothing. If you apply DEET to your child's exposed skin, use it sparingly. Do not apply DEET directly from the container to your child's skin. Apply it to your hands, then put it on the child. Absolutely avoid using it around your child's eyes, nose, and mouth. Do not put it on the hands of small children or on cuts, wounds, rashes, sunburns, or any other skin condition.

Do not allow young children to apply repellents themselves. After returning indoors, wash your child's treated skin with soap and water, and wash all treated clothing. If you believe you or a child is having an adverse reaction to a repellent containing DEET, wash the treated area immediately and call poison control or your pediatrician. Store DEET and other repellents locked out of the sight and reach of children.

Don't Let the Sun's Rays Get to Delicate Skin

Overexposure to the sun's ultraviolet (UV) rays not only causes a painful sunburn but can lead to other serious health problems, including melanoma, a life-threatening form of skin cancer. In fact, as little as one or two blistering sunburns during childhood may double the risk of melanoma later in life. Moreover, excessive UV exposure can lead to premature aging of the skin, nonmelanoma skin cancers, and immune system suppression. These effects, however, may not appear until later in life. It is estimated that people get 80 percent of their lifetime sun exposure by the age of 18.

A child's skin burns more easily than an adult's, and an infant is particularly vulnerable, so infants 6 months and younger should be kept out of direct sunlight altogether. If you can't avoid the sun, make sure your child wears a wide-brimmed hat and lightweight long pants and long-sleeved shirt. Keep her stroller or carrier shaded. The AAP says, however, that when adequate clothing and shade are not available, parents can apply a minimal amount of sunscreen to small areas, such as the infant's face and the back of the hands. Always consult your pediatrician for more information.

Danger in the sun is not limited to the risk of sunburn. Because infant skin does not sweat effectively, a baby is more susceptible to heatstroke. Exposure to the sun may increase the child's risk.

Whenever possible, limit sun exposure for all children during the peak hours of 10 a.m. to 4 p.m., when rays are the strongest. Use sunscreen that is at least SPF 15 and is broad spectrum (protecting from both UVA and UVB rays). Be sure to choose one made especially for babies, which will make an allergic reaction to the sunscreen less likely. If your child is aged 6 months or older, liberally apply the sunscreen to his skin before he is dressed—at least 30 minutes before he goes outside. Choose a water-resistant or waterproof sunscreen if your child will be in the water. Reapply it every 2 hours, as well as after your child has been in the water or towels off. Consult instructions on the bottle. Use sunscreens all year round and even on cloudy or cool days. UV rays can penetrate the clouds, and it is possible for skin to burn even if neither you nor your child feels warm. Extra precautions should be taken near sand, snow, concrete, or water, which can reflect up to 85% of the sun's damaging rays.

Make sure there is shade in your backyard. If you don't have trees that will do the job, you can create your own shade using tents or canopies. Clothing that covers your child's skin helps protect against UV rays, so have her wear a hat and lightweight, long-sleeved, full-length clothing when possible and practical. Cotton fabrics are a good choice, and it's best to use a tightly woven fabric—one that when held up to the light, little shines through. Look for wide-brimmed hats (not baseball caps) that shade your child's face, scalp, neck, and ears. Consult your pediatrician at once if an infant under the age of 1 is sunburned, or if any of these symptoms are present: a fever, fluid-filled blisters, or severe pain.

Remember That Sunglasses Are As Important As Sunscreen

Long-term exposure to UV radiation increases the risk of sight-stealing conditions such as cataracts and macular degeneration. Children are more susceptible to UV exposure than adults because the lens in their eyes is clearer. As one ages, the lens yellows and tends to block more UV to the back of the eye. The feature you should demand when you choose sunglasses is that they have 100 percent UVA and UVB protection. There are a variety of sizes to fit a baby as young as 6 months; don't buy toy sunglasses. Like sunscreen, sunglasses need to be worn on cloudy days as much as on sunny days.

Home Playground Equipment

Keeping your child safe can be tricky if you want to have playground equipment right in your own backyard. It is a sad fact that each year about 200,000 children are treated in U.S. hospital emergency rooms for playground-equipment-related injuries. (An estimated 51,000 involve home playground equipment.) About 15 children die each year as a result of playground-equipment-related incidents; half of the deaths are related to home play settings. Most of these injuries are the result of falls, and most of the deaths reported each year are due to strangulation.

However, there are guidelines to help you make sure your child does not suffer a serious injury and can still have fun. Before allowing your child to touch any play equipment, check for hot surfaces. Hot metal from which you quickly draw your hand away can seriously burn your child's delicate skin.

Get Playground Equipment That Is Right for Your Child's Age and Weight

Don't buy equipment expecting your child to grow into it. If the child is too small for the equipment, he cannot safely use it. Many injuries of young children occur when they play on equipment designed for older children. How do you know if the equipment isn't suitable? If your child cannot reach or use the equipment by himself, it is wrong for him. Start with age-appropriate equipment and add to it in stages, as the child grows. Swings should be composed of soft materials, such as canvas or rubber, and no more than two swing seats should be suspended in one section. The American Society for Testing and Materials (ASTM) sets standards for playground equipment. No matter what equipment you buy, be sure it has an ASTM F 1148 label.

Choose the Site Carefully and Install According to the Manufacturer's Instructions

As you plan your yard, keep spacing in mind. Find a place in your yard that is at least 6 feet from walls and at least 7 feet from electrical wires, and prepare this area so that it is nearly level but will drain. Follow carefully the manufacturer's instructions for installation and anchor the equipment well. Each single apparatus should be set at least 12 feet from every other structure. Many backyards don't have this much space. If you purchase a home that has playground equipment already installed, be sure the site meets the above requirements.

Several times every month, inspect your playground. Look for splintering, cracks, or signs of wear. Be sure bolts are tight and every piece of equipment is anchored properly. If any equipment is broken, repair it or remove it. Rake the surfacing and remove debris, then check the surfacing depth. Add more surfacing where necessary.

Provide a Soft Landing

Install a cushioning product over an adequate fall zone. The material should be under and around every swing, every slide every piece of equipment. It should reach at least 6 feet in all directions from each stationary apparatus. For swings, it should extend—at the front and back—as far as twice the height of the suspending bar. Twelve inches of loose fill material such as sand, pea gravel, wood products, or loose rubber products will make a soft-enough cushion, but you can also use rubber or synthetic mats, which require less maintenance. Rubber and synthetic mats must be tested by the ASTM F 1292-04 standard. (Make sure you see the results in order to know how thick the mat needs to be in relation to the height of the equipment.) Do not use asphalt, concrete, dirt, grass, or soil; they are not safe. Whatever material you use, maintain both the surface and the equipment on a regular basis.

Don't be tempted to get plastic play sets or climbing equipment for indoor use, either, without providing a soft landing. Surfaces such as wood, tile, or cement floors, even if they are carpeted, cannot absorb enough shock from a fall. Plastic play sets and any climbing equipment should be used on shock-absorbing playground surfaces (such as rubber mats) to prevent head injuries.

Limit the Height of Play Equipment

Limiting the height of play equipment is a primary way to prevent severe injuries from falls. For preschool children, the highest rung or platform on any climbing equipment or the top of a slide should be 4 feet or lower. Provide equipment that has openings less than 3 1/2 inches or more than 9 inches. The spaces between ladder rungs present the most common entrapment hazards, but the openings in guardrails or platforms should also be measured. Children usually go through an opening feet first. If the space is big enough for a child's body but too small for his head, he could strangle.

Dress Your Child in Playground-Safe Clothes

Do not let your child wear anything around her neck that might snag on equipment. This includes oversize clothing, as well as necklaces or scarves. Remove drawstrings from outer attire. In cold weather, use neck-warmers instead of scarves. Closed-toe shoes, such as sneakers, are safe; sandals are not. However, you must make sure laces are tied well enough that they will not come loose and trip the child or get caught in play structures. Do not allow your child to wear a bicycle helmet while on playground equipment. It can get caught on equipment and cause strangulation. A jump rope is also dangerous on the playground. Do not attach a rope to playground equipment and make sure none of the children in your yard use a rope on the playground equipment.

Conversely, be sure there are no points on the play equipment that can catch a child's clothing. A child can strangle to death if he becomes entangled in small spaces. Check especially the top of slides, the S-hooks on swings, and the joints of climbers.

Help Your Child Learn the Rules of Playground Safety by Showing Her How to Use the Equipment

Even in your own backyard, there must be safety rules, and you'd rather your child not learn them the hard way. Make sure your child uses any equipment the way it was intended to be used. Make sure she knows how to do it, and explain the dangers of not following the rules. At first she won't understand, but by following the example you set when you are with her, she'll learn almost automatically.

- When someone else is on the swing, walk far behind it.

- Do not play close to a moving swing.

- Do not play at the bottom of a slide.

- Etiquette is good to practice as well: Wait your turn, and don't push or shove.

Supervise!

Be an active supervisor. Stay close to your child and watch as she plays. This requires your full attention.

Note: Playground Equipment is made for children ages 2 to 5 and 5 to 12. A standard for play equipment for children ages 6 months to 2 years of age is scheduled to be published by ASTM in 2005. Playground equipment for public use (at child care centers, schools, and parks) should meet the ASTM F 1487 standard.

Playground equipment in eating establishments follows the ASTM F 1918 (soft, contained play equipment) standard.

The Family Barbecue

There will come a day when the youngest member of your family is roaming around the yard at a family barbecue. You have already made sure the grill was put together according to the manufacturer's instructions, and you are following your owner's manual regarding the way you use it. Now exercise caution. Your child will be attracted to the smell and sight of food cooking, and because the grill is relatively low to the ground, it is within his reach. Never leave a heated grill unattended and always carefully supervise your child around it. Keep pets, as well as children, away from the grill, especially when it is lit and for hours after, while it is still hot to the touch. With all that, you must also be alert to using the grill with food safety in mind.

Keep Children at Least 3 Feet Away From a Hot Grill

Establish a 3-foot zone, but just in case adults become distracted, the child should be taught never to touch hot coals—make that any coals. They may look cool, but coals stay hot long after they have become gray in color. Keep matches, lighter fluid, charcoal, propane, electrical starters, and cooking utensils out of reach. Also, lock the grill when not in use.

Remember the Importance of Bacteria Control in Cooking

Watching out for harmful bacteria is just as important outside as it is in the kitchen. It is a good idea to have two sets of barbecue tongs, so that the one used for putting the raw meat on the grill is not used for taking cooked meat off. Of course, if you have only one set, you can wash the tongs thoroughly while the meat is cooking.

The Swimming Pool

A swimming pool may provide family fun and exercise, but it is one of the most dangerous single areas inside or outside your house. A fact stated in Chapter 4, "Bathroom Safety," is worth repeating here: Drowning is the second leading cause of unintentional injury-related death among children ages 1 to 14.

Install Safety Devices to Restrict Access to the Pool

The more barriers and devices, the better. When a child is missing, each device gives the parent additional time to locate the child. The best safety device is a 4-sided isolation pool fence. It should be 5 feet high, with no footholds, around the entire perimeter of the pool. Do not use the house as one of the sides, since access to the pool from the house is a major factor in drowning incidents. In addition, the fence should be completely separate from the play area and yard.

Another important safety feature, a must for your pool, is a system of gates and latches. Only gates that are self-closing and self-latching will do. That way you'll never wonder if you locked the gate—and you'll never forget! The latch function is defeated if you prop open the gate to the pool area. Don't let anyone do that, including service people. If a pool or lawn care company comes to your home, emphasize to the manager, as well as to the technician, the importance of always securing the pool gate.

All gates should open away from the pool, and their latches should be out of reach of children. Move furniture away from the fence so your child can't climb up to reach the latch or climb over the fence. Inspect the gates and latches often and be sure they are in good working order. All doors leading to the pool area—not just the gates on the pool fence—should have child-resistant locks and be self-closing, if possible.

Installing audible alarms on the doors, which will let you know when someone leaves the house, will notify you when your child goes outside and might be heading for the pool. Adding an alarm on the fence itself is also a good idea.

In conjunction with a pool fence, a pool cover may be used. However, pool covers are not designed to prevent children from drowning. As with all other pool equipment, you will want to follow the manufacturer's directions for safe use, installation, and maintenance. When the cover is in place, keep it locked, and never leave a pool cover partially in place; a child can be trapped underneath. Here's that reminder again: A child can drown in an inch of water! Keep that in mind and drain any standing water from the surface of the cover.

Make Sure the Pool Is Safe

Read and carefully follow all operating and maintenance instructions furnished by the pool manufacturer, as well as those for pool equipment and chemicals. Remember to store pool supplies and chemicals locked out of the sight and reach of children. Even when you're sure you're doing everything right, inspect the pool and equipment regularly. If you find anything amiss, have a professional make any necessary repairs.

In the pool, as in the bathroom or anywhere else in the home, water and electricity do not mix! Keep electrical appliances (including telephone wire) away from the pool and make sure any electrical outlets near the pool are covered. If an appliance must be near the pool, make sure it has a ground fault circuit interrupter. If at all possible, use battery-operated appliances. On the subject of electricity: Don't allow swimming during a thunderstorm. Swimming during inclement weather should be forbidden always, but this is so especially when there is lightning.

Routinely inspect drain covers to be sure they are in place and are not cracked or missing. A missing, askew, or broken drain cover can cause serious injury to children because of the drain's strong suction action. Dual drains are recommended. This minimizes the suction of any one drain, reducing risk of death or injury. Replace drain covers with antivortex covers. (Some states require them for all commercial and residential pools and spas.) Without such covers, a person can be held underwater when her hair, an arm, a leg, or part of her torso becomes entrapped in the drain. Do not allow your child in a wading pool unless it is equipped with a securely attached antivortex drain cover. Any swimmer with long hair should tie it up or wear a bathing cap to prevent becoming entangled in a drain cover. Show everyone where the cutoff switch for the pump is located and teach your child to stay away from the drains.

The deck, too, can present hazards. In addition to keeping electrical appliances away from the pool area, any breakable objects such as glass should not be used. The deck should be clear of any objects that children may trip over.

Learn These Lessons for Life

The American Academy of Pediatrics recommends that you wait until your child is at least 4 years old to start swimming lessons. It is thought that 4 is the age when children are developmentally ready for swim lessons. In addition, children under age 4 are more likely to develop infections from swallowing too much water and can also develop a serious condition called water intoxication. Parents can get started earlier with classes in which kids learn to keep their heads above water. Infant and toddler aquatic programs are very popular among parents and kids and a great way to teach your child to enjoy being in the water. Such classes also teach parents how to keep their children safe around the water.

Such programs can be valuable, but don't let them lull you into a false sense of security. They do not decrease your child's risk of drowning and are not a substitute for adult supervision and safety in the water. In whatever class you enroll yourself and your child, make sure the instructor is certified by Red Cross or YMCA standards and that classes are conducted in pools that comply with current standards for design, maintenance, operation, and infection control.

Always—Carefully and Constantly—Supervise Your Child Around Water

There is no such thing as "drown-proof." Constant eye contact and active supervision is required when children are in and around water. Never leave them alone, not for one second. Any time children are in or around water, a responsible adult must be there, watching carefully. Don't multitask while supervising: no reading, napping, or talking on the telephone. The adult who supervises should know how to swim and know how to administer CPR. The American Academy of Pediatrics recommends that whenever infants or toddlers are in or around water, an adult should be within arm's length, providing "touch supervision."

Do not use air-filled swimming aids in place of life jackets or life preservers with children. Such aids can give parents and children a false sense of security, which may increase the risk of drowning. These air-filled aids are toys and are not designed to be personal flotation devices. Air-filled plastic tubes can be punctured or unplugged inadvertently, causing them to deflate quickly. Remember, no device is a substitute for adult supervision.

Children should always wear a U.S. Coast Guard approved personal safety device around oceans, rivers, and lakes, and always when participating in water sports. During social gatherings, designate an adult as a water watcher to actively supervise children around water. When parents become preoccupied, children are at risk. When swimming at public swim areas, allow your child to swim only if there is a lifeguard, but do not rely on that person to personally supervise your child. The lifeguard has too many children to watch to be able to give one child individual attention.

Safety can often be a matter of good manners. Teach your children never to run, push, or jump on others around water.

Take Precautions after the Swim

Teach your children to take all their toys out of the pool at the end of pool time. Make sure all toys have been removed so there will be no enticement (in addition to the water itself) to get back into the pool or the pool area. Before leaving the area, make sure the gate and pool cover are locked. Keep other playthings and tricycles away from the pool area all the time; a playing child could fall in. To signal that pool time is over, take off your child's swimsuit immediately after the swim. If the pool is a wading pool or an inflatable pool, empty it after every use and place a tamperproof cover over it, or store it upside down and out of children's reach. For an aboveground pool, remove the steps before leaving the area.

Be Prepared for an Emergency

Learn infant/child CPR and first aid and have your babysitters and anyone else who cares for your child learn it, too. In addition, instruct caregivers about potential hazards to your child in and around swimming pools, impressing upon them the need for constant supervision. Keep these rescue equipment items near the pool: a U.S. Coast Guard approved life preserver and ring buoy, with a line securely attached, and a long-handled hook to assist or retrieve a victim from the water. Also, keep first aid kits on hand and post CPR instructions near the pool.

Keep a portable phone at poolside, so you won't be wasting precious time in an emergency. Have emergency numbers affixed to the portable phone. (See the "Form for Emergency Numbers" section in Chapter 14, "Preparing for Emergencies.")

Make an emergency plan. The first step is having a clear view of the pool from your home, even if it requires the removal of trees, bushes, or other obstacles. If you ever turn around and find that your child is missing, every second counts. Before you look anywhere else, check your pool or spa. If a child is missing from the pool area, check the pool first. Go to the edge of the pool and scan the entire body of water, bottom and surface, as well as the surrounding pool area.

Become familiar with the pools in your neighborhood. Inspect all of them, as well as those at the homes of relatives or friends whom you frequently visit. Make sure they are properly fenced off and the gates are kept locked.

Take the Same Safety Precautions with Hot Tubs and Spas

Hot tubs and spas can be as dangerous for children as swimming pools and should be regarded with the same degree of caution. Apply the same important safety rules you've read above. In addition, a locked safety cover should be used for your spa.

A young child should not use a hot tub or spa, for her lighter body weight and developing organs make her much more sensitive to the stress caused by higher water temperature. The water in a spa is hot enough to damage her delicate skin, as well. Consult with a pediatrician before allowing any child to use the hot tub. In addition, anyone sensitive to high temperatures should consult a physician before using a hot tub or spa. This includes pregnant women, diabetics, heart patients, or anyone taking prescription medicine.

Spa temperatures should never exceed 104° F.

DO IT YOURSELF!

Practice good hygiene.

- Don't allow your child to swim when she has diarrhea. This is especially important for kids in diapers. They can spread the germs into the water and make other people sick.

- Always wash your child thoroughly (especially his bottom) before swimming. We all have invisible amounts of fecal matter on our bottoms that end up in the pool.

- Teach your child not to drink or swallow water from a pool or any recreational waters.

- Take your child on bathroom breaks or check diapers often to lessen the chance of a fecal accident in the water.

- Make sure you and all family members bathe or shower with soap and water before swimming. Thoroughly wash your child's hands, as well as your own, with soap and water after using the bathroom or changing diapers.

- Diaper changing should be performed only in the bathroom, never at poolside.

Follow the Rules for Healthy Swimming

Never allow your child to swim in any recreational water that does not meet health standards. Fecal accidents can result in the spread of infectious disease. Germs such as cryptosporidia can survive for days in chlorinated water, and E. coli 0157:H7 bacteria are killed only if chlorine is at proper levels. If your child accidentally swallows contaminated pool water, he can become infected. These germs can cause stomachaches and diarrhea; in some cases, they can be deadly. It's best to avoid taking your family to wading pools or water parks where diaper-aged children go into the water.

Review and Safety Checklist

- ✓ Keep your garage, workshop, and basement off-limits for your child, and use high dead bolts or flip locks to help enforce the rule.

- ✓ Store flammable liquids such as gasoline in safety-approved containers outside the home, in a well-ventilated, locked shed or detached garage and away from any source of ignition.

- ✓ Keep poisons, such as antifreeze and windshield-wiper fluid, locked away out of the sight and reach of children.

- ✓ Lock up or remove entrapment hazards, such as coolers and storage chests, and store all buckets upside down.

- ✓ Keep children away from outdoor power equipment.

- ✓ Keep grass cut short, remove unwanted vegetation, and get rid of stagnant water around your home.

- ✓ Perform a head-to-toe tick inspection on your child after every outing when the temperature has exceeded 40°F.

- ✓ Use extreme caution with repellents, carefully following label instructions. Do not use DEET on babies younger than 2 months. Consult your pediatrician for specific recommendations before using DEET on your child.

- ✓ When possible and practical, protect your child from bug bites, ticks, and sunburn by dressing her in brimmed hats; lightweight, long-sleeved shirts; and long pants (avoiding bright or floral patterns). Tuck clothing into pants and pant cuffs into socks.

✓ Infants 6 months or younger should be kept out of direct sunlight. For children over 6 months of age, liberally apply sunscreen with an SPF of at least 15, at least 30 minutes before your child goes out. Use sunscreen and sunglasses (with 100 percent UV protection) year-round, even on cloudy or cool days.

✓ When purchasing and installing playground equipment, make sure it is appropriate for your child's age and weight. Choose the playground site carefully, and provide soft landing material beneath and around all equipment.

✓ Dress your child in clothing that is safe for the playground (nothing loose or dangling), and teach your child the rules of playground safety.

✓ Keep children at least 3 feet away from a hot barbecue grill.

✓ If you have a home swimming pool, install a 4-sided isolation fence at least 5 feet high and equipped with self-closing, self-latching gates. Prevent direct access from a house or yard to the pool or spa.

✓ Install pool equipment according to the manufacturer's instructions and inspect and repair equipment on a regular basis. Take special care with the pool drains; use antivortex covers.

✓ Never leave a child unsupervised in or around water, and never rely on any pool flotation device or swimming lessons to protect a child.

✓ Learn CPR and keep rescue equipment, a telephone, and emergency numbers poolside.

✓ After every session in the pool, remove all toys, lock all latches, and drain inflatable and wading pools. Store them upside down.

✓ Take the same safety precautions with hot tubs and spas as you do with swimming pools. In addition, do not allow a young child to use a hot tub or spa.

Safety with Pets

The only little bundle that might come close to warming your heart as much as your baby does is a squirmy puppy or a soft kitten. A child can learn some wonderful life lessons while caring for a pet, but there are potential hazards that accompany pets of any kind. A very young child can harm your pet, and a pet can most certainly harm your child. If you have both a baby and a cat or dog, never leave them in a room alone together. If you do not have a pet already in your home when your first baby is born, postpone getting one—for the sake of the pet, as well as your child. It's best to wait until your child is at least 5 years old before getting a pet. Children under 5 will not always understand or remember instructions. In any case, always make sure you take your time, choosing a pet carefully. Supervise children around pets and teach children how to act around other animals. You can prevent injuries by careful choice, supervision, and education.

Steps to Take If You Already Have a Pet

If you already have a pet in the household, I highly recommend that you consult both your veterinarian and your pediatrician about specific concerns.

Work with a Veterinarian

Regular veterinary visits for your pets are important for the health and safety of everyone in your family. Dogs and cats should be appropriately immunized and kept on flea-, tick-, and worm-control programs.

Keep Your Pet from Causing Injury

• Spay or neuter your dog. Not only will the pet have fewer health problems associated with its reproductive system, but she will also be calmer and less likely to bite.

• Enroll your dog in an obedience training class. (Ask your veterinarian for recommendations.)

• Trim your dog's nails regularly and keep your cat's nails trimmed short and dull. You may want to consider declawing your cat if he tends to scratch.

• Keep your pet's food, water, and toys away from your child. Not only can pet food be a choking hazard, but ingesting some pet foods may be a health hazard for children. The water dish is a drowning hazard. Remember, if it has an inch of water, your child could drown in it. The pet's toys have germs, and even if your baby doesn't put them in her mouth—fat chance!—she'll get the germs on her hands, which will, without a doubt, go in her mouth.

> **DO IT YOURSELF!**
>
> *Safety Check*
>
> • Never leave a baby or young child alone with any pet.
>
> • Keep the baby's room off-limits to your pet. Install a safety gate or screen door.
>
> • Always supervise children around dogs, cats, and other animals.
>
> • Keep a pet's food, water, and toys away from your child.
>
> • Keep all pet supplies locked away and out of children's sight and reach.

• Avoid using chemical tick and flea collars or flea dips. Choose nontoxic alternatives.

If You Already Have a Dog, Prepare Him for Your Baby's Arrival

Nearly half the dog bites seen in emergency departments have happened with the family pet in the child's own home. That's why it is very important to take steps to prepare your dog for the newborn's arrival.

- Get the dog used to baby sounds before the infant arrives. Prepare an audiotape of a baby crying (your friends can help with this), and play it for the dog.

- Consider using a toy baby doll to help your dog get accustomed to a real baby. Engage in routine activities, such as feeding, diaper changing, and holding the "baby." Take the dog out for a walk with the doll in a stroller to find out how he will react. You'll have time before the baby comes to teach the dog to behave appropriately.

- Before the baby comes home from the hospital, allow the dog to sniff items the baby has used, such as an undershirt or blanket. That way the dog will become familiar with the baby's smell and be less curious when the newcomer arrives.

If You Already Have a Cat, There Are Some Facts You Should Know

Even before your baby is born, your cat may be a potential source of harm. Your cat or kitten can bring into your home a disease called toxoplasmosis, a flulike illness caused by a parasite named Toxoplasma gondii. Generally known to be transmitted through raw meat—especially pork—toxoplasmosis can also be transmitted through cat feces. If you are healthy and do not have

DO IT YOURSELF!

Guard against toxoplasmosis.

- If you already have a cat, clean your cat's litter box with care.

- If you are pregnant, let your spouse do it!

- If you are pregnant and must change the litter box yourself, wear gloves and change the box on a daily basis. The parasite found in cat feces needs only 1 day after being passed to become infectious.

- Immediately wash hands thoroughly with soap and water after cleaning the litter box.

- If possible, avoid contact with soil and sand. If you must have such contact, wear gloves when gardening and handling sand from a sandbox. Wash hands well afterwards.

- Follow all food safety guidelines outlined in Chapter 3, "More about the Kitchen."

an immune disorder, you can have the disease without knowing it because the symptoms can be mild. If you are pregnant and become infected with toxoplasma for the first time, during or just before your pregnancy, you can pass the infection on to your baby. The disease can cause birth defects such as mental retardation, liver and spleen damage, and visual impairment or blindness, especially if the fetus becomes infected in the first trimester.

For more information about toxoplasmosis, contact your health care provider. Consult the veterinarian to learn more about your cat's risk for toxoplasmosis. To help prevent your cat from becoming infected with toxoplasma, always keep indoor cats inside. Feed cats only dry or canned commercial cat food. Never feed cats raw meat because this can be a source of toxoplasma infection.

Safe Practices around Animals

Teach Your Child How to Act Around Animals
Even if your home doesn't have a pet, teach your children these safety tips for when they are around animals in others' homes.

Always . . .
- treat animals with kindness and respect

- handle pets gently

- wash your hands thoroughly after handling pets

Never . . .
- approach any unfamiliar animal

- disturb an animal that is eating, sleeping, caring for its young, or guarding something

- touch any pet before asking its owner if it is okay to do so

- tease, chase or stare at an animal

- grab an animal by the feet, ears, or tail

- touch or pick up a wild or stray animal

- try to break up animals fighting

- play with a dog unless supervised by an adult

Also show your child what to do if approached by an unfamiliar dog:

- be still like a statue if a dog comes up to you

- if you're knocked down by a dog, roll into a ball and lie still like a rock

Turn this lesson into a game by role-playing.

Practice Sanitation and Good Hygiene

Animals can be a source of illness for people, and people may be a source of illness for animals. Following basic sanitation practices is essential to maintain the safest possible environment for both the pets and the children in your care.

- Everyone—children and adults—should wash their hands after handling pets, pet foods, or pet wastes. Thorough hand washing with soap for at least 20 seconds using warm, running water has been effective in preventing disease transmission.

- Keep pets and their living quarters squeaky clean. Dispose of animal waste immediately. Animal cages should be of an approved type with removable bottoms for easy cleaning.

- Clean up animal feces in the yard immediately. Keep the cat's litter box out of a child's reach and cover children's sand boxes when not in use to prevent cats from using them as litter boxes.

Watch for Ticks

Ticks carrying Lyme disease can be carried into the house by any pet that is allowed outside. Any animal that gets into your yard can carry ticks. Your household pets cannot directly transmit Lyme disease to anyone in your family, but loose, infected ticks on pets can be a hazard for people around them. Ask your veterinarian for advice about which tick control product is best for your pet. For more information about ticks, see Chapter 6, "Safety in the Backyard."

Keep the Fish Tank Off-Limits

Put the fish tank in a place where children cannot climb up on it, fall in it, or pull the tank over on themselves.

Remove Pet Reptiles from Your Home

Reptiles such as iguanas and turtles have become popular as household pets, even though these creatures are particularly likely to carry Salmonella bacteria. Most healthy adults and older children who are infected with Salmonella will recover within a week from its diarrhea, fever, and abdominal cramps without any serious side effects. However, infants, young children, and anyone with a suppressed immune system is likely to suffer severe or fatal illness from such an infection. These bacteria can be transmitted easily to children through a reptile's feces, which may stick to its body or cage. Without careful hygiene—washing hands thoroughly with soap and water after handling the reptile or after cleaning its cage—the fecal material can be ingested or can contaminate any items (such as a pacifier) with which the child's mouth or hands come in contact.

For this reason, children under 5 years of age and people with weak immune systems should avoid contact with reptiles. Remove pet reptiles even before the infant arrives. Persons should always wash their hands thoroughly with soap and water after handling reptiles or reptile cages.

Obviously, reptiles should not be in day care centers.

Completely Avoid Having Certain Exotic Animals as Pets

Avoid exotic pets such as monkeys, spiders, and venomous or aggressive snakes, as well as wild animals such as raccoons, bats, and skunks. Your veterinarian or doctor can answer questions about any pet health risks for children and adults in your family.

DO IT YOURSELF!

Keep your pet clean.

- Regularly shampoo pet bedding, rugs, carpets, and furniture coverings.
- Vacuum often—everywhere the pet has gone.
- Bathe your pet and its sleeping areas regularly, using soap, not detergent.
- Clean cat litter trays daily and keep out of the reach of children.
- Dispose of pet waste immediately.

Prevent Rabies

Rabies is a serious viral disease that attacks the brain and other nervous system tissue. Although it is almost always fatal if left untreated, the good news is that immediate protective treatment (thorough cleaning of the wound and the vaccine regimen) is effective in preventing the disease from developing. It is true that common carriers are wild animals such as skunks, bats, foxes, and raccoons; however, dogs and cats can be infected with rabies, too. Any infected mammal can transmit rabies to humans, either through a bite or by the animal's saliva or nervous tissue entering an open wound or mucus membrane (that is, eyes, nose, or mouth).

To help protect your family from rabies, be sure to vaccinate your dogs and cats against it. (Ferrets need to be vaccinated, too.) Avoid contact with wild animals and unfamiliar dogs and cats. Do not feed or handle wild animals or strays. Report strays and wild animals that appear sick to your local animal control agency so that they can be captured. Teach your children to enjoy watching wildlife from afar.

DO IT YOURSELF!

Learn to recognize the signs of rabies.

You cannot tell if an animal has rabies just by looking at it, but there are signs of rabies that can alert you. Be suspicious if . . .

- a wild animal appears tame

- a nocturnal animal is seen in the daytime

- any animal exhibits nervous or aggressive behavior

- any animal is foaming at the mouth or drooling excessively

Take Immediate Action If a Family Member Is Bitten or Scratched by an Animal

If your child or any family member is bitten or scratched by any animal, act quickly. Wash the wound thoroughly with soap and water for at least 5 minutes and seek medical attention immediately.

Be aware that a bat that has bitten someone does not always leave a bite mark. If you see a bat in a room with your child, seek medical attention.

Review and Safety Checklist

✓ Wait until your child is 5 years old before getting a pet.

✓ Never leave a baby or young child alone with any pet.

✓ If you have a pet, regular veterinary visits are important for the health and safety of everyone in your family. Dogs and cats should be appropriately immunized and kept on flea-, tick-, and worm-control programs.

✓ Keep the baby's room off-limits to your pet. Install a safety gate or screen door.

✓ Always supervise children around dogs, cats, and other animals.

✓ If you are pregnant and must change the litter box yourself, wear disposable gloves and change the box on a daily basis. Wash hands thoroughly afterward.

✓ Remove pet reptiles from a household where children under 5 years old reside.

✓ Completely avoid certain exotic animals as pets.

✓ Stay away from strays and report them to your local animal control agency.

✓ Teach your child to enjoy watching wildlife from afar.

✓ Take immediate action if a family member is bitten or scratched by an animal.

Fire Safety

In a typical year in the United States, more than 3,000 people—a quarter of them children aged 14 and younger—die in home fires. Don't become part of those statistics. Take a 4-step approach to fire safety at home:

- remove potential fire hazards and correct unsafe practices

- install and maintain smoke alarms

- acquire equipment to help you fight and escape fires

- and devise and regularly practice an escape plan.

Four Steps for Safety

Remove Potential Fire Hazards and Correct Unsafe Practices

For this step you'll begin outside the house. Keep your roof, gutters, and outside property areas of your home clean and free of debris (such as leaves and garbage) that could feed a fire. Inside and out, keep matches, lighters, candles, and other heat sources locked away out of children's sight and reach. Playing with matches is the leading cause of fire deaths for children ages 5 and under, so teach your children that matches are tools, not toys. Your child learns that he should never use his dad's drill, and he can learn the same rule for matches. Children as young as 2 years old are capable of lighting cigarette lighters and matches, so it's a good idea to combine teaching with keeping matches and lighters out of reach—no matter how obedient your toddler seems to be. Discard any lighters that are not child-resistant, but remember that child-resistant is not childproof.

If there is a smoker in the house, another hazard and another set of rules must be considered. Never smoke in bed or when you are drowsy. Don't leave a lit cigarette unattended in the ashtray and always use deep, sturdy ashtrays. Make sure cigarettes are properly extinguished before emptying the ashtrays. Even cigarette butts can ignite trash. Better yet, encourage smokers to go outside; an added benefit will be that your child will be kept away from harmful secondhand tobacco smoke.

Burning candles is another safety hazard that is easily addressed—avoid using them as long as small children are in your home. In addition to the special instructions found in Chapter 15, "Debra's Holiday Safety Guide," there are some general rules to follow no matter what the age of family members:

- never use candles near draperies or anything else that might easily catch fire

- do not allow children or teens to have candles in their bed-rooms

- never leave candles unattended.

Candles stored for emergencies or other special needs should be locked away out of the sight and reach of children.

Anyplace where fire is used as a tool, extra precautions must be taken, and the room in which this happens most is the kitchen. You may wish to go back to Chapter 2, "Preventing Injuries in the Kitchen," to review ways to avoid burns and unwanted fires there. Anywhere in the house, if you are going to be standing or walking near a stove, fireplace, or open space heater, do not wear long, loose-fitting garments, for they are more likely to catch fire than short, fitted clothing.

A space heater should be used with caution. Place any such unit at least 3 feet away from walls, upholstered furniture, drapes, bedding, rugs, and other combustible materials. And be sure to read and carefully follow the manufacturer's instructions regarding use of the heater. Don't leave space heaters turned on when you leave a room or go to sleep. Never leave a child or pet alone with a space heater; stay close to supervise.

Use the same kind of smart approach with your fireplace. Employ a professional chimney sweep to inspect and clean your home's chimney and fireplace annually. Unless you are trained to do this work, it should not be considered a do-it-yourself project. Maintenance is crucial, for creosote builds up in chimney flues and can cause a chimney fire. Once your fireplace has been inspected and cleaned, continue to use caution. Use a sturdy fireplace screen in front of any open flame.

> **Cleaning your chimney or fireplace . . .**
>
> **Not!**
>
> Employ a professional for this job.

Think about heat sources when you choose a place to store flammable material. All flammable liquids such as gasoline, paint thinners, and kerosene should be kept in properly labeled, tightly closed, safety-approved containers. These products should be stored out of the reach of children, outside the house in a locked shed or detached garage. Keep them in a well-ventilated place away from any source of ignition and always take the containers outside to fuel power mowers and other equipment.

In Chapter 4, "Bathroom Safety," being careful with electric appliances and cords was considered, but there are some issues left to be mentioned. It is important to inspect electric appliances and cords on a regular basis. Replace frayed extension cords and appliances that have worn or loose connections. Do not overload electrical outlets, even though some items you use will make additional plug-ins available. And do not run electrical cords under carpeting or hang them from nails or doors. Those cords should not be treated as casually as a rope or piece of twine. You could get the shock of your life—literally.

Your great grandma may have had to wait for a sunny day to do the family laundry, but all that changed with the widespread use of the electric or gas clothes dryer. This common, everyday appliance can cause a fire if not properly attended. Check your dryer's exhaust duct (usually a tube that runs from the back of your dryer to a wall vent). If it's made of plastic, replace it with metal, which won't burn if lint lodges inside and catches fire. If the duct is metal but is crushed or bent, replace it. This will eliminate a place where lint could build up. Carefully follow the manufacturer's maintenance procedures and be sure to clean the lint filter after each use. Go out and remove any obstructions around the exterior vent cap, and trim shrubbery to maintain at least 12 inches of clearance. One more thing: Do not leave home with your dryer running unattended.

Despite all these precautions, a house might still catch on fire. Never leave young children home alone or unsupervised—not even for a few minutes. Dress your children for bed in sleepwear that is made from flame-resistant materials. Look for garments made from 100 percent polyester, which is inherently flame-resistant and does not require chemical treatment. Sleepwear (larger than 9 months, up to size 14) must be flame-resistant or snug-fitting to meet CPSC sleepwear requirements. Do not put children to sleep in loose-fitting T-shirts or other oversize clothing made from cotton blends. These garments can catch fire easily. Loose-fitting clothes stand away from the body, which makes contact with an ignition source more likely. Loose-fitting clothing allows an air space next to the body that helps keep the fire burning.

Carefully follow washing directions on the label. Many fabric softeners carry a warning not to use them on children's sleepwear. That's because repeated use of a fabric softener can cause some 100 percent cotton fabrics to burn faster.

Install and Maintain Smoke Alarms

Smoke alarms are your family's first line of defense against fires. These devices sound a loud alarm to warn you in time to escape a fire. They can cut nearly in half your family's chances of dying if you have a fire. Many of the deaths and injuries suffered in a fire are actually caused by smoke and poisonous gases because they rise ahead of the flames. Even when you are awake, you might not see a fire until after the smoke or gas claims a life in your home.

The first thing to do, then, is purchase a smoke alarm. (Because smoke alarms are required by law in many localities, check with local codes and regulations before you purchase one.) Battery-operated smoke alarms cost from $7 to $25, depending on their features, and can be purchased at your local discount or hardware store. Electrical smoke alarms with battery backup systems are excellent choices for your safety protection. These alarms, which can cost from $25 to $30, are hardwired into your home's electrical system. These should be installed by a qualified electrician.

Even if you hire someone to do the hardwiring, you should be ready to help with placement. Both you and the electrician should read the manufacturer's instructions in order to carefully follow them. Many fire departments will come to your home and offer advice on proper installation; some will provide smoke alarms free to families in need.

Installing smoke alarms isn't the end of the matter—they must be maintained. Every single alarm in the house must be in working order. Test each one monthly, whether battery-operated or hard-wired. Replace batteries in all smoke alarms once a year. An easy way to remember to change them is to do it in the spring or fall when you change the clocks. If an alarm chirps between those times, change the battery then, too. Follow the manufacturer's instructions. If remembering to change a battery isn't your forte, use a 10-year lithium battery. Never remove a battery from the smoke alarm to use even temporarily in another battery-operated item, such as in your child's toy. Clean the alarm regularly to keep it dust-free. Replace the alarm every 10 years.

DO IT YOURSELF!

Install smoke alarms in all the right places.

- Read and carefully follow the manufacturer's instructions.

- Place each wall-mounted alarm 6-12 inches below the ceiling. Place ceiling-mounted alarms at least 6 inches from any wall.

- Place alarms away from air vents, windows, doors, fireplaces, or high air flow. Do not place a smoke alarm in a corner where the ceiling meets the wall.

- Avoid placing smoke alarms in kitchens or bathrooms where cooking fumes, steam, or exhaust fumes could trigger false alarms.

- The National Fire Prevention Association Code requires new homes to have interconnected smoke alarms on every level, outside each sleeping area and inside each bedroom. Although this approach is ideal for all homes, existing homes, at a minimum, should have smoke alarms on every level—including the basement—and outside each sleeping area.

- If you have an older home in which the smoke alarms are not interconnected, a baby monitor in the nursery will allow you to hear the alarm in that room no matter where you are in the house. If you have smoke alarms that operate on your household electrical current, you can have them interconnected so that every alarm sounds, regardless of the fire's location. (Be sure to use battery backups for hard-wired alarms.)

- Don't decorate your smoke alarms; paint or stickers may keep them from working properly.

Acquire Equipment to Help You Fight and Escape Fires

Purchase multipurpose extinguishers and install them in the kitchen, basement, and workshop area. Put them in plain view but out of reach of your children. Take the time to learn how to operate the equipment before an emergency strikes. Use the extinguisher only for small, confined fires. While you are extinguishing a small fire, have other family members exit the home and telephone the fire department.

Consider purchasing an automatic fire sprinkler system so that a fire will be attacked in its early stages. A system like this sprays water on the area where fire is detected. It is less costly to install such a system when a house is under construction, but it can also be installed in an existing home. Used in conjunction with smoke alarms, a sprinkler system is extremely effective in protecting your family from fire.

Another safety product that you may not have considered is an escape ladder. In making the purchase, look for a noncombustible ladder that bears the mark of an independent testing lab. Make sure the ladder can support the heaviest person in the home. Don't bring it home and put it on a back shelf in a remote closet. It will do little good there. Store the ladder close to a window so that if it is needed, you can get to it quickly, hook it onto the window sill, throw it down, and climb out.

A plan is only as good as the execution. Become totally familiar with the manufacturer's instructions on how to safely use the ladder, and make sure each family member knows how to use it properly. Show older children how to attach the ladder and tell them, in case of fire, to back out the window to climb down. Take the ladder out of the box and set it up, but do not actually practice the drill of climbing down from a second-floor window (or higher), since there is a risk of falling while practicing.

Devise and Regularly Practice an Escape Plan

Even though you should avoid practicing with the ladder from a high window, there are some drills that will help your family survive in case of a home fire. Map out at least two escape routes from every room in the house. One way out is the door; the second way out may be a window. Always keep these routes clear, and be sure windows designated as fire exits have not been painted or nailed shut. Also, see that windows or doors with security bars are equipped with quick-release devices.

Practice your escape route with all family members at least twice a year. Because a house filled with smoke can frighten and disorient family members, it is critical to have an emergency plan that everyone in the family understands. The extent to which you include your children in these discussions depends on the age and level of maturity of each individual child. A toddler will be able to comprehend a little. Your infant will just be along "for the ride," but be sure to include her during practice. As your child grows and understands more, you will need to update your family escape plan. Know when he is ready to escape without your assistance. You will need to practice with him so that he is totally familiar with this plan.

Because the most deadly fires occur at night, it is a good idea to conduct your fire drills at night. Sound the smoke alarm as part of the practice session. If you live in an apartment, become familiar with the building's evacuation plan and, in case of fire, remember to take the stairs, not the elevator. Decide in advance which parent will be responsible for helping each young child out of the house. Designate a place outside the home where family members will meet, such as beside a specified lamppost. This will allow you to be sure everyone is safe.

Even small children, with practice, can understand the directions in the sidebar. You'll also need to prepare your children for seeing a firefighter, helping them understand what the firefighter is there to do. Even though firefighters are

DO IT YOURSELF!

Teach your children essential fire survival skills.

- Get out fast and stay out. Do not hide in closets or under beds or in any other area inside the home. Call 911 from a neighbor's house and never go back into the burning house for any reason! Reinforce with your child that he must not stop or return for anything, such as a toy or pet. Never go back!

- Stop, drop, roll—if your clothes catch on fire, stop. Drop to the ground right where you are; roll over and over and back and forth to smother the flames; cover your face with your hands.

- Feel a door with the back of your hand before opening it. If the door is warm, do not open it (use an alternate exit); if the door is cool, open it slowly and proceed with caution. Move quickly to the nearest exit.

- Crawl low on your hands and knees under the smoke, where the air is safer to breathe.

Practice these skills!

seen regularly on television shows and have been lauded for their courage in the aftermath of the 9/11/2001 disaster, seeing a firefighter up close can still be scary for a child. Explain to her that firefighters need to wear protective clothes to keep them from getting burned. They use equipment to help them breathe, protecting them against smoke inhalation. Although firefighters may look like aliens from another planet when they come to fight a fire, they will be there to help protect the family. Show her a picture of a firefighter in full regalia or take her to your local fire station for a tour.

If you are trapped in a burning building, close all the doors between you and the fire. Line the doors with towels or clothing (ideally, they should be damp) to keep the smoke from coming into the room. If there is a phone in the room, call 911 or the fire department. If there is no phone in the room, go to the window and signal for help by waving a bright-colored cloth or shining a flashlight.

The rules for fire safety should be applied everywhere your children visit. When your child is ready, make a game of having each child apply the rules to the school, library, movie theater, and friends' homes. Make sure your child knows at least two ways to get out of any building. Teach him to be fire smart.

Review and Safety Checklist

✓ Remove potential fire hazards from your home and use caution with all flammable products.

  ✓ Clean debris from around your home and keep lighters and matches locked away.

  ✓ Properly extinguish cigarettes and never leave lit cigarettes unattended.

  ✓ Use space heaters with caution.

  ✓ Periodically have the fireplace cleaned by a professional.

  ✓ Store flammable material away from heat sources.

  ✓ Periodically inspect electric cords and appliances.

✓ Carefully follow the manufacturer's maintenance procedures for your dryer. Clean the lint filter after each use and never leave the house while it is running.

✓ Dress the children for bed in flame-resistant clothing. Do not put children to sleep in loose-fitting cotton garments.

✓ Install and maintain smoke alarms.

✓ Acquire escape and fire-fighting equipment.

✓ Devise and regularly practice an escape plan.

✓ Teach your children fire survival skills.

Gun Safety

The first and most important rule of gun safety is this: Remove all guns from places children live and play. Although as a parent, as well as a safety expert, I implore you to choose not to keep a gun in your home, I realize that some parents prefer to have guns. Even if you do not have guns in your home, you must realize that other parents have made a different decision. This chapter is for all parents, because if your child visits a home where a gun is kept, you (and she) need to know some basic rules.

For Parents Who Keep Guns

If you absolutely must have a gun, make sure you keep it under lock and key. Literally. If you keep a gun at home, follow these safety guidelines, which all experts agree can save lives.

Store Gun Components Out of Reach and Out of Sight
Keep the unloaded firearm in a locked gun cabinet, safe, or gun vault. Ammunition should be locked away in a separate location. Keep the keys to these cabinets in a place to which your child does not have access.

Use a Child Safety Lock
Children have been known to thwart all best efforts, so a second system should be followed for extra protection: Install trigger locks or other safety devices to prevent the unauthorized use of a firearm. Make sure each gun lock is made of metal and comes from a reputable company. Never use a lock with plastic parts. Do not use a trigger lock on a loaded gun, which can discharge even with

the lock on. Don't think it is just older children you need to protect. Even children as young as 3 years old are strong enough to pull a trigger.

Incidentally, air guns, BB guns, pellet guns, and paint guns should also be kept out of children's hands. Thousands of children aged 14 and under are treated in hospital emergency rooms annually for nonpowder, gun-related injuries.

For Parents Who Don't . . . As Well As Parents Who Do

Quiz Your Friends

Nearly half the homes in America have firearms. Ask the parents of your children's friends and relatives—anywhere your children may visit—if they own a gun. Don't allow your children to visit there unless you are certain the gun is stored unloaded and securely locked away.

Teach Your Child

Every child from preschooler to teen should be taught that guns and other weapons can hurt and kill people. Teach them this rule: If you see a gun, don't touch it; get away and tell a trusted adult. Follow the same rule if you see any other kind of weapon or dangerous instrument, such as a syringe.

Teach your young child the difference between a toy gun and a real one. Before age 8, few children can reliably distinguish between real and toy guns or fully understand the consequences of a fired gun. Children watch TV and movies and see people using guns. Explain to your child that the gun in the story is not real and the people are just pretending to be shot by the gun. Help your child understand that in real life, guns do kill people. Unfortunately, verification for that lesson is in the newspaper every day.

If you wish to provide more security for your family in the face of violence in our society, there are more effective ways than bringing a gun into your house. Invest in a home security system; unlike a gun, it cannot be used against you or members of your family. You can also organize or become involved in a neighborhood watch program. When your youngest child is at least 5 years old, consider getting a dog whose bark can scare away intruders. Consult with a veterinarian regarding the best dog for your family.

Review and Safety Checklist

- ✓ If you have guns in your home:

  - ✓ Store guns and ammunition in separate locations, and keep all components locked out of reach and out of sight of your children.

  - ✓ Install trigger locks or other safety devices to prevent unauthorized use of your guns.

- ✓ Whether or not you keep a gun in your home:

  - ✓ Anywhere your child goes, ask the adults there if they have guns. Make sure everyone who has guns follows the guidelines above. If they do not, you should keep your child away.

  - ✓ Teach your child the difference between a toy and a real gun, and teach him to tell a trusted adult if he sees a gun. Teach him not to touch a real gun.

Common Poisons
in the Home

Toddlers are particularly prone to unintended poisoning. They have been putting stuff in their mouths all of their short lives, but now they can get to all those wonderful mysteries under their own steam. Each year poison control centers across the U.S. report more than 1.1 million children under the age of 5 are exposed to potentially poisonous medicines and household chemicals. The best way to keep your child from ingesting poison is to keep all potentially harmful products out of sight and out of reach, in cabinets that have locks or child-resistant safety latches. Bear in mind that a child can figure out ways to get to the tallest shelves. Keeping intriguing articles out of sight is an important safety component. Taking these precautions may become second nature to you in your own home, but your awareness of such possibilities is important in homes you visit, too. Studies show that 30 percent of pediatric poisonings occur due to children's ingestion of their grandparents' medications.

It is ironic that products we bring into the house to help our children can be toxic to them. While medicine created especially for children may not be considered a poison by most folks, the wrong dosage can kill. (This is true, as well, for adults.) When giving medicine to your child, don't just read the label and decide it's the right thing for a specific situation. Check with the pediatrician first. Once you have her approval, carefully follow directions on the label—dosage is likely to be based on weight and age—and use the measuring dispenser that comes packaged with the medication.

Another way we may bring in toxic substances is to wear them on our clothes. Family members who work with poisonous materials should shower, if possible, and change clothes and shoes before leaving work. This reduces the possibility of your carrying toxins from the workplace into your car or home.

Poisonous Products in the House

Guard Against Mistaken Identity

Teach your children to always ask permission before eating or drinking anything, and store harmful products away from food. Never put harmful products side by side with food and keep all products in their original containers. Any family member might ingest something that you have transferred to a milk jug, jar, or 2-liter bottle, mistaking the contents for something meant to be consumed. Moreover, labels on original containers will assist medical caregivers or personnel at poison control centers in the event of a poisoning.

The same rules apply to medicines, vitamins, and supplements. Something that is good for adults may be poisonous for children. For example, although iron supplements are safe for adults who follow label instructions, ingestion of only a few of them can be lethal to young children, depending on the amount of iron per tablet and the weight of the child. Simply putting these items on a high shelf in the kitchen or in the bathroom medicine cabinet is not safe. Keep all medicines—both prescription and over-the-counter—as well as vitamins and supplements in a locked cabinet out of the reach of children. If you keep medications or any other potentially harmful products in your handbag, don't leave it within reach of any child. Remember this precaution when

> **DO IT YOURSELF!**
>
> *Avoid mistaken identity.*
>
> - Never store poisonous products in a refrigerator or pantry.
>
> - Keep everything stored in original, correctly labeled containers.
>
> - Keep all poisons—including all medications—locked out of sight and reach of children.
>
> - Never call medicine candy.

you visit in a home that has children or when you have visitors in your home. If Aunt Polly comes to visit and puts her purse on the floor beside her chair, cheerfully tell her you are putting her purse in the same place you keep yours, which is out of the sight and reach of children.

After you have used any medication—even aspirin, diet pills, or vitamins—securely close the child-resistant cap and promptly return it to its place. Once again the mantra: Child-resistant does not mean childproof! Remember to never call medicine candy. In addition, because young ones tend to imitate adults, avoid taking medicines in front of children.

Keep All Cleaning Products Out of Your Child's Sight and Reach

Like medicine, there are poisonous products that are good when used as intended. Just as we take precautions with fire, we must take care with poisonous products. Many household cleaning products are toxic. Using these products incorrectly endangers the health of your family and the air quality in your home. Improper storage may lead to unintentional poisoning. Improper disposal can pollute our drinking water.

Start being careful from the very beginning—in the store. Buy water-based products when possible. Select the least toxic product you can find and avoid purchasing products labeled Danger or Poison; typically they are the most hazardous. When you must buy products containing hazardous substances, buy only the amount you expect to use, and use it as soon as possible.

Before using the product, make sure you read the labels and follow those directions carefully. Wear protective equipment, such as gloves, as recommended by the manufacturer. Never mix cleaning products or chemicals unless directions indicate you can safely do so, especially ammonia and bleach, which together produce a toxic gas. Use products in a well-ventilated place; open windows and use a fan to circulate the air toward the outside, and keep children away from the area. Close the product lid as soon as the product is used. Do not re-use empty household cleaning product containers. Purchase household cleaners in child-resistant packaging and always re-close it properly. Store all cleaning products— even less toxic ones—in a locked cabinet or cabinet secured with child-resistant safety latches.

Practice preventive measures. When there is a spill, clean it up as soon as possible, before it has time to set, thus cutting down the amount of cleaner needed. Before using so-called air fresheners that simply cover odors, try airing out the house. Use liners to catch spills. Protect yourself, too, by not smoking or eating while using poisonous products.

Even in safe homes where products are carefully stored, poisoning can occur when the product is taken out of storage and is in use. Therefore be extra cautious when using harmful products around children.

Make Your Own Cleaning Products

The most toxic household products are corrosive or caustic cleaners. They contain lye or acids, and they are found in drain cleaners, oven cleaners, and toilet-bowl cleaners. They are the most dangerous cleaning products to have around the house because they can burn skin, eyes, and internal tissue at the slightest contact. Using homemade products is a tradition in my family, passed from my grandmother to my mother to me. Here are some do-it-yourself alternatives to highly toxic products:

Instead of:	Use:
Drain cleaner	A plunger or plumber's snake.
Oven cleaner	Steel wool and baking soda; add salt for tough stains. (Not recommended for continuous-cleaning ovens and self-cleaning ovens.)
Toilet bowl cleaner	Toilet brush and baking soda or vinegar. (This will not disinfect.)
Glass cleaner	1 tbsp. vinegar in 1 qt. water. Spray on and use newspaper to wipe dry.
Furniture polish	1 tsp. lemon juice in 1 pt. vegetable oil. Wipe on, then off.
All purpose cleaner	4 tbsp. baking soda in 1 qt. warm water. Apply with sponge (or paper towel if meat, poultry, or seafood juices are present) and rinse with clear water.

Use only recipes obtained from reputable sources, and don't concoct your own brews. If you have any questions about mixing products together, call the product manufacturers to find out if they recommend the mixture or if there are hazards associated with using their products in some nonprescribed manner. Safe storage is required even with homemade products, and they must be labeled. Note the exact ingredients and the purpose for the product. You think you'll remember, but in a month or two—trust me!—you will not recall what is in that unlabeled container. In choosing a container, never put your homemade products in a milk jug, cup, or 2-liter bottle.

Be Aware of Dead Ringers

Some poisonous products look exactly like foods and drinks our children commonly ingest. Even an older child or an adult can easily make a mistake and unintentionally ingest such products, so take special care to securely store them away after use. Some examples are chocolate laxatives or calcium supplements that look like candy bars, pills that look like candy, clear lamp oil that looks like bottled water, and colored lamp oil that looks like mouthwash.

Alcohol

Keep Alcohol Away from Children

Children are much more sensitive to the toxic effects of alcohol than adults. Alcohol can cause a child's blood sugar to plunge to a dangerously low level, which can lead to seizures, coma, and even death in a young child. In addition, keep out of the reach of your children any alcohol-laced products, such as:

- mouthwash (read the label—the alcohol content of these products varies significantly with different brands)

- perfume, cologne, or aftershave

- vanilla extract and lemon extract

- cough/cold medications

- rubbing alcohol

- and antifreeze and windshield-washer fluid.

Poisonous Plants

Recognize Which Plants Are Poisonous

Some of the plants that are used to beautify your house and yard may be toxic, so it's important to identify all the different plants both in and around your home. Because several different plants may have the same common name, find out both the botanical and common name. A list of common poisonous plants can be found in Appendix B.

Obtain a list of the common poisonous plants that grow in your area from the poison center or your local cooperative extension agent. You can also take the plant or a cutting to a reputable and experienced nursery, florist, or plant store for identification. Make a list or put a label on every plant so that, in case of ingestion, you will have pertinent information available.

Your child, attracted to a plant's color or shape, may put parts of it in her mouth, perhaps swallowing it. Symptoms that may occur when this happens include:

- skin, eye, and mouth irritation

- breathing problems

- allergic reactions

- stomach or other pain

- vomiting and diarrhea.

Use Only Nontoxic Plants During Your Child's Early Years

I recommend that you purchase only nontoxic plants when you have pets or children under the age of 6. Toxic plants outside the home should either be removed or fenced in. Inside the home, hang plants from the ceiling. (Choose lightweight pots and secure them with a closed fastening device.) But still keep an eye out for fallen leaves. Even in the case of nontoxic plants, a child may ingest soil, which may contain pesticides or fertilizer. Further, a child can choke on any leaf, even a nontoxic one.

If Aunt Polly brings a plant with her as a gift, ask her what it is. Ignore her raised eyebrows when you tell her you like to label all your plants. "Aunt Polly, this is so lovely. I want to hang it from the ceiling where everyone can admire it. Yes, Aunt Polly, it may be hard to water it up there, but I don't mind at all!"

Reinforce with your children the rule that they should not eat or put into their mouths any leaves, stems, flowers, twigs, wild berries, mushrooms, or any parts of shrubs or garden or ornamental plants. Keep an eagle eye on your child after rainy weather, when wild mushrooms are abundant.

First Aid Tips and Emergency Measures

Be Ready to Reach Poison Control Quickly

Remember this telephone number: 1-800-222-1222. It's the National Poison Hotline. Call it from anywhere in the U.S., day or night, seven days a week. You will be connected automatically to your local poison center. Prominently post this number on every phone in the house. (Call now for free phone stickers.)

Your best bet is to always call the poison center before calling your doctor because you are more likely to talk to an expert right away at the Poison Hotline. You may need to wait for a call back from your doctor. However, if the situation appears life threatening, call 911. In all other cases, calling poison control will enable you to speak to a specialist who can assess the severity of the situation.

Prioritize Your Actions When You Suspect Poisoning

If poison is swallowed:

1. Check your child's mouth and carefully remove any remaining poison.

2. Call the Poison Hotline before administering anything by mouth. Call as soon as you suspect a poisoning; do not wait until symptoms are displayed.

3. Bring the ingested product (or its container) to the telephone when you call the Poison Hotline and take it with you if you must visit the emergency room or doctor's office. If a poisonous plant is the cause, refer to the label you made or the list you keep and take the information with you.

Do not induce vomiting—doing so often makes the situation worse. When you call the poison hotline, you will talk to a specialist who can tell you the correct treatment to administer. The American Academy of Pediatrics currently recommends that syrup of ipecac no longer be used routinely as a home treatment and that parents should safely dispose of the syrup of ipecac currently in their homes.

If poison gets into the eye:
1. Flood the eye with lukewarm (never hot) water. Pour the water from a large glass held 2 or 3 inches from the eye. Continue for at least 15 minutes.

2. Call the Poison Hotline.

If poison gets on the skin:
1. Remove any contaminated clothing and flood skin with water for 15 minutes.

2. Wash gently with soap and water, then rinse.

3. Call the Poison Hotline.

If poison is inhaled:
1. Immediately bring the person into fresh air.

2. Call 911 if the victim appears short of breath.

3. Open doors and windows wide.

4. Call the Poison Hotline.

Poison Patrol Checklist: What to Look For

In the house and yard:
• cigars, cigarettes, butts, ashes, and matches

• plants and plant food

- batteries

- broken plaster

- paint chips and older, repainted toys (may contain lead—see next chapter for details)

In the kitchen:
- window and counter cleaners

- dishwasher products, detergents, soaps

- oven cleaners

- drain cleaners

- ammonia

- cleanser and scouring powder

- carpet and upholstery cleaner

- furniture polish

- pet products such as flea and tick collars and powders

- vitamins and medications, including aspirin

On the table:
- green or sprouted potatoes (they contain a toxin called solanine, which can cause gastrointestinal problems)

- table salt (as little as half a teaspoon to an infant or a table-spoon to a toddler can cause damage to the central nervous system)

In the bathroom:
- cosmetics

- all grooming products

- baby powder and baby oil

- shampoos

- hair straighteners and relaxers

- hair dyes

- hair removers

- creams

- nail polish and polish remover

- deodorants

- perfumes, colognes, aftershaves

- suntan lotions

- mouthwash

- fluoride toothpaste (ingesting large amounts—most or all of the tube—may cause symptoms of fluoride toxicity; use a pea-size amount of toothpaste for children under 6)

- medications, both prescription and over-the-counter, including aspirin, vitamins, and iron pills

- rubbing alcohol

- jewelry cleaner

- toilet bowl cleaners

- disinfectants

- room deodorizer

In the garage, basement, and storage areas:
- pest control products

- weed killers and fertilizers

- gasoline and car-care products such as antifreeze, motor oil, and windshield-washer solution

- turpentine, paints, and paint thinner

- pool supplies

- kerosene

- art and hobby supplies

- glues and adhesives

- charcoal lighters

Note: The main ingredient in many major antifreeze brands is ethylene glycol, which is very toxic. Antifreeze has a sweet taste. Children or pets will drink large amounts of it if it is left out in open containers or if it is spilled in your garage or on your driveway. There is a less-toxic alternative. I recommend that you purchase what I use: antifreeze formulated with propylene glycol. It does not contain the sweet taste that is prominent in conventional antifreeze, making it less attractive to children and animals.

In the laundry room:
- soaps and detergents

- bleach

- fabric softeners

- stain remover

In closets:
- moth balls

- shoe polish

In bedrooms:
- aspirin and other medicines

- perfumes and colognes

- room fresheners

In handbags:
- cosmetics

- aspirin and other medicines

Make sure poison prevention precautions are taken in all the places your baby frequently visits, such as the homes of grandparents, other relatives, and friends.

Review and Safety Checklist

✓ So that you won't mistake one product for another, leave all products in their original, labeled containers. Even with those labels, you should never store harmful products in a refrigerator or pantry.

✓ Read labels carefully. Select the least toxic product you can find whenever possible and always try to buy water-based products.

✓ When using toxic substances, keep children away. Protect yourself, too, by not smoking or eating when using any kinds of toxins.

✓ Remember: Out of reach and out of sight for all medicines, cleaning products, alcohol, and other harmful products. Keep them locked away from young children at all times.

✓ Follow recipes from reputable sources when making your own cleaning products and carefully note all ingredients and the purpose of the concoction. You're making these products for safety's sake, but they can be toxic if ingested or handled improperly.

✓ As long as you have pets or have children under the age of 6 in your home, use only nontoxic plants.

✓ On every phone in your home, prominently post the Poison Hotline phone number: 1-800-222-1222.

✓ Prioritize your actions when you suspect poisoning.

Environmental Hazards

You cannot always depend on your nose and eyes to tell you when something is poisonous. Four toxins examined in this chapter—lead, arsenic, radon, and carbon monoxide—are invisible and odorless. Another, secondhand smoke, is a toxin that can be seen and smelled—by nonsmokers. As any reformed smoker knows, the odor of cigarette smoke clinging to skin, clothing, and fabric in the home can be nauseating. However, the dangers secondhand smoke poses, especially for children, go far beyond that kind of discomfort. Another class of poison, pesticide, is brought into the home deliberately when it is deemed necessary to eliminate harmful pests. As we consider these products, we shall weigh their benefits against the potential harm they introduce. And we'll discuss some less toxic methods for ridding the home of harmful pests. Finally we'll go back into the nursery, this time to consider what harmful chemicals may lurk there and what to do about them.

Lead

The brains and nervous systems of young children are quite sensitive to the damaging effects of lead. Indeed, because lead is more easily absorbed into the growing bodies of fetuses, infants, and children, they are more vulnerable to lead exposure than adults. This danger has not gone away. Lead continues to be a serious health risk for children, even though the CPSC banned the use of lead-based paint for residential use in 1978. The reason is simple: lead does not break down naturally; it stays in the environment until it is removed. This insidious hazard cannot be seen, tasted, or smelled, and children with dangerous levels of lead in their blood may appear healthy. Because lead can pass through a woman's body to a fetus, pregnant women should limit their exposure to lead.

High levels of lead can cause convulsions, coma, or death. Exposure to low levels of lead can harm a child's brain, nervous system, blood cells, and kidneys, which in turn can cause learning disabilities, slow development, hearing impairment, and hyperactivity. Since most children do not display any symptoms, the only way to know for sure if they have elevated lead levels in the blood is to have them tested.

The primary sources of lead poisoning in children today are lead-based paint and lead-contaminated dust. Lead-based paint is usually not a hazard if it is in good condition. However, problems occur when the paint peels or flakes off into chips or lead dust. The same kind of danger occurs when remodeling, renovation, or repainting is performed improperly, without safeguards to control lead dust. Your child doesn't have to eat paint chips to be poisoned. If she touches lead-contaminated dust, then puts her hands in her mouth, the lead will enter her system. Limiting your child's exposure is the best defense. If you suspect your home has lead paint, there are steps you can take to reduce the risk.

Your child is at risk for lead poisoning if . . .

- Your home was built before 1950 or your child frequently visits a home or child-care facility built before 1950.

- Your home was built before 1978 or your child frequently visits a home or building constructed before 1978, if that building was recently remodeled or has peeling or chipping paint.

- The child has a sibling or friend who now has or once had lead poisoning.

- You or any other adult living in your home works with lead.

If you believe your child has been exposed to lead, speak with your pediatrician or health department. A blood test can detect levels of lead in your child's body.

Watch Out for Peeling Paint and Wash It Away

- Keep an eye out for peeling paint or water leaks. Water leaks and moisture are the main cause of peeling paint. Sticking doors and windows can also damage paint.

- Make sure the peeling paint is promptly and safely repaired by someone trained in lead-safe work practices.

- Wash your baby's hands and face before meals, naptime, and bedtime. Teach and reinforce this washing practice with older children, too. Hands contaminated with lead dust are as sure as clean hands to go into the mouth.

- In addition to washing bottles and pacifiers each time they fall on the floor, wash toys and stuffed animals, too.

- Regularly wash floors and high wear-and-tear areas such as window frames, window sills, doors, and door frames, and anywhere your child plays. Vacuum first. High Efficiency Particulate Air (HEPA) vacuums work best. Change the bag and filter according to the manufacturer's instructions. Contact your local health departments—some have a HEPA vacuum loan program. Then use a wet mop with a mild detergent to get all the paint chips and lead dust. Hint: Use two mop buckets—one for soapy water and one for rinsing. Change the rinse water often.

If Your Home Was Built Before 1978, Get Your Home Professionally Tested

This is especially important if you plan to remodel or renovate. Many consumers find spot kits helpful as an initial screen for the presence of lead, but while they give instant results via changes in color, they are not as reliable as laboratory tests. Two types of professional testing are lead inspection and lead-risk assessment. An inspection discloses the lead content of every surface in your home, but it does not reveal either the level of danger or how you should proceed. An assessment tells you if lead is present and makes recommendations for how the lead can be controlled.

If Lead Must Be Removed, Don't Do It Yourself

Removing lead is best left to professionals. Do not attempt to remove lead paint yourself. Hire a certified lead-abatement contractor. You are risking your own

> *Removing lead . . .*
>
> *Not!*
>
> Leave it to professionals.

health if you remove lead improperly, and you may spread even more lead dust around your home. Make sure your family and your belongings are protected from lead dust. Plan to move out if the project is major or if it generates lots of dust.

Check the Soil in Your Yard and Take Appropriate Measures to Keep Lead Out

Exterior lead paint may have contaminated soil close to the house. Also, if your home is near a road that has seen a lot of traffic (and, thus, exhaust fumes) over the years, your soil may be contaminated from past use of leaded gasoline. Here's what to do if your soil is tainted with lead:

- Cover lead-tainted soil with grass sod, pine bark mulch or gravel, or plant bushes.

- Encourage your child to play in grassy areas that are lead-free.

- Have everyone remove their shoes before entering the house.

- Make sure you wash your child's hands after he has played outdoors and teach him not to eat dirt.

- Don't plant a home garden or serve food that has been grown in lead-laced soil.

Have the Water Tested

Testing your water does not have to be expensive; you can get mail-in kits from environmental laboratories for under $20. (See "Tap Water Safety" in Chapter 3, "More about the Kitchen.") Even if you are on a municipal water system, your pipes may contain lead if your house is old. In homes built before 1988, lead solder may have been used in the plumbing. And leaded brass faucets were not phased out until the period between 1996 and 1998. To find out more about testing, call your local health department or the EPA's hotline. (See Appendix E, "Helpful Resources.")

Stick to Cold Water for Drinking and Cooking

Because hot water is likely to contain higher levels of lead, use only cold water for anything that will be ingested. Run the cold water for 30 to 60 seconds before catching it in a glass, cup, or pan, and if it has been more than 6 hours since you used the tap, allow the cold water to run until it becomes as cold as it will get, which may take up to 2 minutes or more. The longer water sits in your pipes, the higher the risk for lead. Use only cold water for drinking, cooking, or preparing baby formula. Once you have flushed your tap, you can store the cold water in your refrigerator for later use.

If you are concerned about wasting water, catch it in a container and use it for watering your plants or washing clothes. Be sure to clean faucet screens regularly, taking out any solder particles caught by the screens. If there is a high level of lead in your pipes, you may wish to purchase a filter certified for lead removal or switch to a bottled water that is known to be safe for drinking and cooking.

> **Proposition 65-Standards for Lead**
>
> When shopping for dishes, look for lead-free dishes or lead-safe dishes—in other words, those that meet California's Proposition 65. Most tableware in common use does not pose a lead hazard. However, if the amount of lead that can leach into food from your dishes is greater than Proposition 65 levels, your dishes may pose a health risk. Ask the retailer or manufacturer if their product meets those standards or contact the Environmental Defense Fund (see Appendix E, "Helpful Resources ").

Know What Other Products in Your Home May Contain Lead

Some vinyl miniblinds made before July 1996 in China, Taiwan, Mexico, and Indonesia have been found to contain lead. When the plastic deteriorates due to sunlight and heat, lead dust forms on the blinds. If your child wipes her hands on the blinds . . . you know what she'll do. Her hands, and the lead dust, will find their way into her mouth.

Glazes for some dishes and mugs contain lead. Be especially careful when purchasing abroad. If you have a lead-glazed, ceramic container, don't heat, microwave, or serve hot food or drinks in it and don't store acidic foods (such as fruit juices) in it. That lead crystal bottle someone gave your baby is just for show; don't feed your baby with it! Any dish that is meant to be decorative should be just that—don't serve food on it. Silver-plated items or plates made from pewter, brass, or bronze should never be used for serving food to children.

Check Lead Hazards in Other Environments

Day care centers and homes of family or friends that are visited often can also pose a lead hazard. If such homes or buildings were built before 1978, make sure the paint is in good condition. Also, many older school, park, and community playgrounds were painted with lead paint. Ask when the playgrounds were built and look for any signs of chipping paint or dust.

Arsenic

Check Pressure-Treated Wood in and Around Your Home

Arsenic? You may be certain there is no arsenic in your home environment, but think again. Arsenic was once a common ingredient in pressure-treated wood, in the form of chromium copper arsenate (CCA), so it may be in your deck, porch, picnic table, or play set. Arsenic is a known cancer-causing chemical. Long-term exposure to elevated levels of arsenic has been linked to skin, bladder, and lung cancer. Studies show that arsenic can be picked up from the surface of CCA-treated wood. Young children who play on or under structures made of CCA-treated wood and who put their hands in their mouths are at increased risk of exposure. Arsenic-containing residue from the wood can rub off on children's hands while they are at play and be ingested when their hands come into contact with their mouths. Wood treated with CCA is being phased out now, thanks to a 2002 agreement between the EPA and the wood industry to end the manufacture of CCA-treated wood for most consumer applications by December 31, 2003. However, the key words here are *phased out*. There may still be some stocks of wood treated with CCA found on shelves after that date. And certainly if you have items in your yard that were bought previously, your child may be at risk.

If your child has contact with CCA-treated wood, immediately wash his hands thoroughly with soap and water, especially before eating. The sidebar explains what you can do to protect your child.

DO IT YOURSELF!

What to do about arsenic . . .

- Find it. Some CCA has a green tint, but testing is the only way to know for certain. Test kits are available. See Appendix E, "Helpful Resources," to learn how to obtain a test kit. (You may be able to contact the structure's manufacturer or builder to determine if it contains CCA-treated wood.)

- Seal it. Use a penetrating deck treatment. CPSC and EPA are presently conducting studies of coatings and sealants to determine effective measures of reducing the amount of arsenic released from CCA-treated wood. Contact CPSC or EPA for more information. See Appendix E, "Helpful Resources."

- Replace it. High-exposure areas, such as handrails and steps, should be replaced with nonarsenic-containing products.

- Avoid it. Keep children and pets away from the soil and spaces beneath and around it, and do not store toys or tools there. Rain will cause the arsenic to leach onto anything beneath the treated product.

- Cover it. An arsenic-treated picnic table should be covered with a tablecloth. Do not eat, drink, or prepare food on CCA-treated surfaces.

- Don't pressure-wash it, and don't use commercial deck-washing products, which can make the arsenic even more toxic. Use soap and water instead, with cleaning tools and rags you can throw away.

- Don't let your child play on any rough wood surface treated with arsenic; the splinters are poison.

Radon

Radon is an invisible and odorless gas that occurs naturally from the breakdown of uranium. It can be found in soil, rock, and air. When breathed outdoors, this gas poses a minimal health risk, but when it becomes trapped in buildings, concentrations build up, which can be cause for concern. If the radioactive decay products of radon get trapped in your lungs, they can damage the live cells lining the lungs. Years of this damage can lead to lung cancer. In the United States radon is a leading cause of lung cancer, second only to cigarette smoking.

How a home was built and what construction materials were used can affect radon levels. Local geology is another contributing factor. Every state has pockets of high radon levels. Because radon levels vary from one area to another, the only way to know a specific home's radon level is to test it. Any home can have a radon problem, no matter its age or condition and no matter whether there is a basement. Homes more likely to have higher levels are those built on uranium-rich soil. Basements and first floors are more likely to have the highest radon levels. It is also possible for your home to have an elevated radon level while a neighboring home does not.

Radon can enter your home through openings around water pipes, gas pipes, sump pumps, and drains. It can also enter through cracks and holes in the walls and foundation. The water supply is another possibility. (See item 2 below.)

According to the EPA, your family's risk of getting lung cancer from radon depends mostly on how much radon is in your home, the amount of time you spend in your home, and whether you are a smoker or have ever smoked. Smoking combined with radon is an especially serious health risk.

Test the Air in Your Home

Because of the serious health threat posed by radon, the Environmental Protection Agency recommends that all residences, except those above the second floor in multilevel buildings, be tested. Fortunately, testing is easy and inexpensive. There are a number of radon kits available on the market that you can purchase through mail order or at your local hardware store. The price range is $10 to $45. It is important that you use detection kits that have passed the EPA's testing program or are state approved. You can perform your own test or you can hire a radon tester in your area that is state certified or proficient with a national radon program. Your state radon office can supply you with a list of testing kit companies and radon testers that have met those standards.

Insist that your child's day care center or school be tested.

DO IT YOURSELF!

Testing for radon . . .

Test kits are either short- or long-term.

Short-Term Kit. 2 to 90 days; the most common is a charcoal canister.

Long-Term Kit. 90 days to a year; the most common is an alpha track detector.

Radon levels tend to vary, not only from day to day but also from season to season. For that reason, a long-term kit—which takes into consideration seasonal variations—is a better test.

Note: Radon is measured in picoCuries per liter of air—pCi/L. Although the EPA says there is no known safe level of radon and that any radon exposure carries some risk, it has set 4pCi/L as the level at which it recommends action to reduce your home's radon level.

If the Air in Your Home Has Radon, Test the Water

If you have tested the air in your home and found a radon problem, it is a good idea to test the water, too. If you are on a public water supply, call the utility company for more information. If your water comes from a private well, contact a lab that is certified to measure radiation to test your water—especially if you live in an area that is known to have high levels of radon in water.

Be Aware That There Are a Variety of Ways to Lower Radon Levels

Don't despair if testing indicates elevated levels of radon in your home. There are a variety of ways to lower radon levels. You can help matters by increasing ventilation by opening windows, doors, and vents on the lower floors when practical. However, this is regarded only as a temporary radon-reduction approach. Radon-reduction techniques—preventing the entry of radon or removing radon and its decay products from the air in your home—should be performed only by a qualified radon mitigation contractor. Your state's radon office can provide you with a list of state-certified contractors and those who are proficient in a national radon program.

If the potential is high for radon in an area in which you plan to build a new home, you can have radon-resistant features installed during construction. If you do this, however, be sure the builder has experience in installing radon-resistant features. The cost for reducing radon levels typically ranges from $800 to $2,500. The average cost to install radon-resistant features during new home construction is $350 to $500.

Carbon Monoxide

Carbon monoxide (CO) is a colorless, odorless, tasteless, and toxic gas created when fossil fuels such as oil, natural gas, wood, propane, or kerosene burn without enough oxygen for full combustion. Motor vehicle exhaust is also a source of this hazardous gas. It is not produced by electric appliances. Any fuel-burning appliance, vehicle, tool, or other device is a potential CO source. When fuel-burning appliances are kept in good working condition, they produce little CO. Malfunctioning, improperly used, or poorly vented appliances can produce fatal CO concentrations in your home.

CO poisoning can occur from inhaling small amounts of CO over a long period of time or from large amounts inhaled in a short time. Unborn babies, infants, and people with anemia or a history of heart disease are more vulnerable to exposure to CO. Breathing low levels of carbon monoxide can cause these flulike symptoms: mild nausea, mild headaches, fatigue, and shortness of breath. Symptoms at moderate levels include nausea, severe headaches, dizziness, disorientation, confusion, and fainting. Breathing higher levels of carbon monoxide can cause loss of consciousness and death.

While many of the symptoms of CO poisoning resemble other illnesses, such as flu or food-borne illnesses, become highly suspicious if more than one family member experiences similar symptoms, if the symptoms occur only in the house, or if symptoms decrease when you leave the house and reappear when you return. Tell the doctor you suspect CO poisoning. It can be diagnosed by a simple blood test.

Install, Inspect, and Use Appliances According to the Manufacturer's Directions

Prevention is the best defense against carbon monoxide poisoning. If you have experience with such work and plan to install an appliance yourself, be sure to follow the manufacturer's instructions and local code. Most fuel-burning appliances should be installed professionally.

> *Inspecting and correcting problems with fuel-burning appliances . . .*
>
> *Not!*
>
> Only a trained service technician can do this. Leave it to professionals.

Follow the manufacturer's directions as well for safe use and operation. (Never use the gas range or oven to heat a room.) Only a trained service technician can detect hidden problems and sources of carbon monoxide and correct them. Have a trained professional annually inspect your gas water heater, gas range and oven, gas dryer, gas or kerosene heaters, fireplace, wood stove, gas swimming pool heater, and your oil or gas furnace (especially before turning on the furnace in the fall). Three activities to NEVER do:

- burn charcoal in homes, tents, vehicles, or garages

- run a car in a garage, even if the garage doors are open

- operate any sort of portable generator indoors, including in homes, garages, basements, carports, crawl spaces, and other enclosed or partially enclosed areas, even with ventilation. Follow the instructions that come with your generator. Locate the unit outdoors and away from doors, windows, and vents that could allow CO to come indoors.

To avoid electrocution, keep the generator dry and do not use in rain or wet conditions. To protect from moisture, operate it on a dry surface under an open, canopy-like structure. Dry your hands if wet before touching the generator.

Look for Leaks and Repair Them Quickly

Repair any leaks immediately. Make certain the flues and chimneys are connected and in good working order and are not blocked. Examine vents and chimneys regularly for improper connections and visible rust or stains. When using a fireplace, open the

---

DO IT YOURSELF!

Never ignore these CO warning signs:

- An unfamiliar smell or burning odor
- A decreasing hot water supply
- A furnace's inability to heat the house or its running constantly
- The appearance of soot, especially on appliances and on the outside of the chimney or flue—indicating that an appliance is not operating properly
- A persistent yellow-tipped flame—indicating that the fuel is not burning efficiently
- Increased condensation on the inside of windows

If you see any of these warning signs that signal a possible CO problem, immediately contact a professional service technician to fully examine the faulty unit.

---

flue for adequate ventilation. Keep gas appliances properly vented and never operate an unvented gas-burning appliance in a closed room. Choose properly sized wood stoves that are certified to meet EPA emission standards. Make sure all doors fit tightly. Install and use an exhaust fan over gas stoves, vented to the outdoors.

Install Carbon Monoxide Alarms

A CO alarm is a device that measures how much CO has accumulated, sounding an alarm before the gas reaches toxic levels. Discount and hardware stores sell CO alarms, which typically range in price from $25 to $60. Select alarms that meet the requirements of the most recent Underwriters Laboratories (UL) 2034 standard, International Approval Services (IAS) 6-96 standard, or the Canadian Standards Association 6.19-01 standard. Look on the package for these designations.

A CO alarm should be installed in every sleeping area and at least 15 feet from any fuel-burning appliances. Read and carefully follow the manufacturer's recommendation for the alarm's placement, use, and maintenance. Remember, a CO alarm should never be a substitute for the safe use and maintenance of fuel-burning appliances. Teach your child the difference between the sound of your CO alarms and that of your smoke alarms.

Know Other Places Where Carbon Monoxide Poisoning Can Occur

There is a risk of CO exposure anytime you are near a fuel-burning device or there are unusual circumstances. For example, snow can block your car's exhaust pipe, causing exhaust fumes to accumulate inside. (Tip: It isn't a bad idea to have your car's exhaust system inspected periodically—snow or no snow.)

Make sure carbon monoxide poisoning doesn't tag along with you when you go on vacation. Follow the rule you follow at home: Don't use any fossil-fuel-burning appliance (such as a gas stove, charcoal grill, or gas generator) in any enclosed space, including campers and tents. The same rule applies on the water. CO poisoning can occur on a houseboat or in any other boat cabin that incorporates the boat's engine. I recommend that CO alarms be installed in your recreation vehicles and boats, as well as in your home.

Secondhand Tobacco Smoke

If there is environmental tobacco smoke in your home, it is a consequence of a deliberate act. This air pollutant, more commonly called secondhand smoke, hurts young children, especially, for their lungs are more susceptible to its harmful effects. Secondhand tobacco smoke contains as many as 4,000 chemicals, more than 50 of which are cancer causing agents. Exposure to secondhand smoke is associated with an increased risk of SIDS, asthma, bronchitis, and pneumonia in young children.

For Your Unborn Baby's Sake, Quit Smoking

If you are expecting a baby, quit smoking. Please. The impact of maternal smoking on fetal development is well documented. According to the Centers for Disease Control and Prevention, the harmful effects include stillbirth, premature birth, low birth weight, sudden infant death syndrome, and a higher rate of infant mortality. The longer you smoke during your pregnancy, the greater the risk. Quitting anytime will help, but the sooner the better.

Even if you don't smoke, you and your children may be routinely exposed to secondhand smoke at work, home, or other regularly frequented environments. Try to protect your entire family by taking the following steps.

- Enforce a no-smoking policy in your home and car. That includes guests, babysitters, and workers. Remember, smoke doesn't just linger in the air in a certain room; it also circulates throughout the house through the ventilation system.

- Encourage all family members to quit. For assistance, seek advice from a doctor, who can refer you to a local smoking cessation program.

- Enroll your child only in a day care center or school that is smoke-free.

- Frequent only public places that prohibit smoking, especially when your child is with you.

- For your own good health, ask your employer to ban or restrict smoking to separate ventilated areas.

Be a role model and behave the way you want your children to behave. Don't smoke around your children (or any child, for that matter). Don't have a cigarette dangling from your mouth. Don't be caught sneaking one. Never smoke around anyone with asthma.

Pesticides

Pesticide is a generic name for a whole class of chemicals intended to prevent, control, eliminate, or mitigate any pest. These include insecticide, herbicide, rodenticide, and fungicide. These products are designed to be toxic. It's a no-brainer that a poison designed to kill one organism may harm other organisms, too. Some pesticides affect humans by causing cancer, central nervous system damage, and respiratory illnesses. Others can have toxic effects on human reproductive, endocrine, and immunological systems. For many pesticides, we don't know what the long-term health effects are.

Because children's brains and their nervous and immune systems are still developing, they may be particularly vulnerable to poison. Depending upon what type of pesticide is involved, ingesting or inhaling even small amounts may result in illness. We, as parents, should be concerned enough to want to reduce or eliminate pesticides. Because there are many effective preventive measures and less-toxic alternatives available, why take risks? Your family will have a healthier place to live because of your precautions. Since prevention is paramount, let's start with that.

Reduce the Need for Pesticides by Eliminating What Pests Need

Like all other creatures, pests need food and water. Eliminate the pests by eliminating what they need.

- Cut off their water supply by reducing humidity in your home (the smallest amount of water is sufficient for a bug) and by repairing leaky faucets. Repair all structural problems. Don't allow water to stand anywhere around the house. When looking for such spots, don't forget water trays under plants or under the refrigerator or air conditioner compressor.

- To eliminate pests' food supply, start in the kitchen. No food (including pet food) should be left out; store all food in tightly sealed containers. Clean up promptly after meals and snacks: sweep up crumbs and mop up spills.

- Institute a family rule: No eating or drinking anywhere in the house other than the kitchen and dining room. Don't allow children to snack in their bedrooms.

- As soon as a meal is over, wash the dishes, empty the garbage, and clean the garbage pail that is kept in the kitchen. Garbage that is set outdoors should be put into cans that are always tightly closed, with no food or other attractants around.

Further Discourage Pests by Eliminating Their Hiding Places

Cleanliness is imperative. Vacuum often, and bathe the family pets regularly. Because cardboard boxes, paper bags, newspapers, and stacks of magazines—including reading material kept in the bathroom—make good hiding places for bugs, try to eliminate such clutter as much as possible. Before bringing paper bags or boxes into your home, inspect them for pests. To be safer, carry your own canvas bags to the store. Then when you hear the question, "Paper or plastic?" you'll be able to say, "I brought my own."

Plug Their Entries

Don't leave windows or doors—including garage doors—open if they have no screens, and install screens on all drains, as well. Drain plugs should be kept in place when water is not draining into the pipes. Every entryway should be blocked, including cracks in the floor and around pipes. Caulk and seal! Any gap or hole is an invitation to rodents, snakes, and stray animals. A mouse can squeeze through a hole through which a pencil can pass, and a rodent can enlarge a hole by chewing.

Use strong metal grates to cover attic vent openings. Holes should be large enough to allow air to circulate, but no hole should be larger than a quarter-inch.

Destroy Pests' Outdoor Homes

Clean up around the outside of the house by removing all debris—including diseased vegetation and leaves. Any animal droppings in the yard should be cleaned up right away. If stacks of wood or boxes are necessary, keep them in sealed containers, as you do garbage. Create a system that promptly drains rain water from your property, and never leave pails or buckets situated so they can collect water, which can also be a drowning hazard. If pests are a problem, replace mulch with fine gravel. Why? Because mulch is organic matter, which attracts pests and provides them with attractive harborage.

Pesticides and other toxins may be carried into your home on the soles of shoes, where they can settle into your carpet, a place where your child plays or crawls. So make sure family members and guests wipe their feet on the front doormat and leave their shoes at the door.

Use Pesticides as a Last Resort and Take Necessary Precautions

Any pesticide stored in your home puts your child at a greater risk for poisoning. In fact, many of these chemicals are as toxic to us and our children as they are to the bugs. That's why pesticides must be locked away, out of the sight of children. (See Chapter 10,

---

DO IT YOURSELF!

Have a bug-free yard without pesticides.

- Develop healthy soil by testing and then doing what is necessary to achieve the right pH, nutrients, and texture.

- Let your grass grow to 2 ½-3 ½ inches in order to choke out weeds. (Don't let the grass grow too long, for longer grass is attractive to ticks and snakes.)

- Select grass that grows well in your climate and choose plants that don't require much water, fertilizer, or pesticides. Don't buy any plants that are toxic to children or pets.

- Water deeply but not often—about an inch per week unless the climate is extremely hot, in which case an inch every 3 days is about right. Consult your county extension agent for the best lawn care regimen in your area.

- Pull up weeds by the roots.

"Common Poisons in the Home," for more information on poisonous products in the home.)

First, read the label, then follow the directions to the letter, including all precautions and restrictions. Buy pesticides that are premixed (to avoid exposure to concentrated products) and use the smallest amount necessary to do the job. If you are pregnant, avoid all contact with pesticides.

Before applying pesticides (indoors and outdoors), remove children and their toys from the area and keep them away until the area is dry or as recommended by the label. The EPA registers every pesticide sold legally in the United States, but such registration does not guarantee safety.

Go After Pests with Less Toxic Methods

If preventive measures don't work, use less toxic tools to fight them whenever possible.

Ants

You can wash away ants in the house with a soapy dishrag. An effective way to keep ants from coming into your home is to use baiting outside. The problem in doing this is the fact that different kinds of ants prefer different baits, ranging from sugar and fat to protein and carbohydrates. However, since they all seek and need water, water-based baits (containing sodium borate as the active ingredient) may be your best bet. You can also look for hydramethylnon and boric acid (please read precautions in the sidebar on page 148) on the labels of bait traps you consider buying. Sweet liquid baits can be put in special holders that are child-resistant, but remember that child-resistant does not mean childproof. Always place baits out of the reach of children and follow the manufacturer's instructions.

> **DO IT YOURSELF!**
>
> *Where the Ants Are*
>
> Flowering plants attract aphids, which in turn attract sweet-feeding ants. To discourage these pests, don't plant flowering plants closer than 6 feet from the outside walls of your house, and don't let any plants or trees touch your house (thus providing a highway into your home).

Fleas

Your pet is usually the culprit who brings fleas into your house. If the pet goes where fleas hang out, it's a foregone conclusion that soon you'll be vacuuming and fussing and fuming over those maddening critters. (See Chapter 7, "Safety with Pets," for tips on keeping your pet clean.) To help keep fleas out of your house, you must first keep them out of your yard. Consider getting some microscopic worms—more politely called beneficial nematodes. These wonderful creatures help control more than 250 pests (including fleas) that begin their life cycle in the soil. Gardening catalogues usually carry them.

For serious flea infestations, consider using diatomaceous earth. This substance is created by crushing the skeletons of prehistoric algae. (I am not making this up!) When insects walk over the glasslike bits, then breathe them in, the sharp pieces puncture their breathing system. This product can be found in garden centers and pest control departments. Avoid the type that contains free silica (which is sold for use in swimming pools); it is harmful to humans.

Before application, thoroughly vacuum the carpet and any furniture frequented by the pet to reduce the flea population. Just prior to vacuuming, put 1 to 2 tablespoons of cornstarch into the vacuum bag. This creates a mini dust storm; the tiny particles of the cornstarch will clog the fleas' breathing holes. During application, follow the label directions on diatomaceous earth carefully.

Hint: You'll have to wear a dust mask when applying, sweeping, and vacuuming. And you must keep children and pets out of the area until you have vacuumed well. Immediately after vacuuming, remove the bag, place it in a strong plastic garbage bag, and dispose of the bag in a tightly sealed garbage can, preferably outside the house. This is very important because flea eggs can still hatch in the bag. In addition, the diatomaceous earth in the bag can become airborne.

Moths

Moths can be repelled somewhat by cedar blocks or chips. Pheromone scent traps will also help you monitor and trap moths. Another way to discourage moths is to avoid putting into the closet any clothes that have not been thoroughly cleaned.

Roaches

Even the cleanest kitchen can be invaded by a cockroach or two. If they have come in with your grocery bags and have not yet set up a colony, you can solve the problem by stepping on them. If the roaches have gotten a foothold, however, reach for the boric acid, which is available in powder form, as well as in bait stations. In whatever form you bring boric acid into your home, it is important to know that it is harmful. While it has a lower toxicity than many other pesticides, neither pets nor people should ingest it. Place or inject the product only in hidden areas, such as wall voids, cracks, and crevices where roaches hide. Apply it only in areas that are inaccessible to children and pets.

Rodents

Instead of putting out poison, use traps for rats and mice, but place traps in areas out of the sight and reach of children and pets.

Termites

Two means for getting rid of dry wood termites are heat (thermal pest eradication) and sodium borate wood preservatives. Both are effective treatments for entire structures and can be used for spot treatments.

If you choose heat, do not try it yourself; this remedy should be applied by a professional. The procedure consists of using equipment that gradually warms wood sections of the structure to 130° F, then holds the temperature for about sixty minutes to eliminate all stages of wood destroying insects. Sodium borate-based wood treatment works on bare wood, protecting it from wood decay and future attacks by termites. You can use it in places where the wood has not been finished, such as in the attic. In addition, it can also be injected into the wood if the wood is painted, varnished, or

---

DO IT YOURSELF!

Use boric acid powder safely to fight roaches.

- Buy it in the pest control department of any home and garden center or the hardware store.

- Look at the label. If it does not say the product can be used for roach control, don't use it for that purpose. Follow the label directions exactly.

- If you have a pest-control professional, ask him to use a blue-tinted product so it can't be mistaken for food, such as flour or sugar.

- Never leave it exposed on countertops or near food, and apply it only where it will be inaccessible to children and pets.

- When using a broom or vacuum, make sure the boric acid is not kicked back into the air.

otherwise finished. For a house under construction, pretreatment with this product will give the home long-term protection from termites and other pests that destroy wood.

Use Integrated Pest Management, Recommended by the EPA

Integrated pest management, an effective strategy for controlling pests, combines a variety of methods: prevention (such as sanitation and structural repair), mechanical measures (such as traps and pulling up weeds by hand), biological controls (such as beneficial predators), and other measures based on knowledge of the pests. It uses regular monitoring to determine if and when treatments are needed, such as sticky traps to monitor insect activity. Toxic chemicals may be used, but only in extreme cases. Even then, the least toxic effective agent is used. Check with your child's day

DO IT YOURSELF!

Investigate before hiring a pest control operator.

- Look for a qualified pest control operator who practices integrated pest management.

- Ask the pest control company/operator for their state license number.

- Contact your state licensing agency (usually the Department of Agriculture) to inquire if the company or operator has any history of violations or complaints by consumers. You will need to supply the company's license number to obtain this information.

- Ask for the service technician's state certification number. Most states require certification.

- Ask for references . . . and check them out.

- Ask to see a current certificate of insurance.

- Inquire about experience. (What type of insect problems has this person previously treated?)

- Ask to see the label of any product being used.

- Be sure to read the product's material safety data sheet; it tells you the active ingredients in the product and gives precautionary warnings. (For additional information about the product, contact the resources listed in Appendix E, "Helpful Resources.")

- Request that chemical pesticides be used only as a last choice for controlling pests.

care or school; ask what pest control methods they use. Request that they use integrated pest management.

Chemicals in the Nursery

Have you ever walked into a room that had been freshly painted or newly carpeted and said, "The room smells new"? For someone who has no chemical sensitivities, this can be construed as a good thing—something like enjoying a "new car" smell. However, a safe, clean room should have no smell at all. You may be surprised that some of the products commonly found in a nursery—carpeting, fresh paint, new or refinished furniture, and cleaning supplies—can "off-gas" or emit toxic fumes called volatile organic compounds (VOCs). VOCs are a range of chemicals, many of which have hazardous properties. Some are carcinogenic and can irritate our lungs. Formaldehyde is a VOC with a pungent odor. (You may remember this smell from the high school biology lab.) It is a widely used chemical in household products.

A child is more susceptible to the adverse effects of toxins than an adult because a child's lungs are smaller, and children breathe more rapidly. Consequently, they inhale more pollutants per pound of body weight than adults. If that air is contaminated, they will inhale more pollutants. Infants are particularly vulnerable. Because an infant's nervous and immune systems are in the earliest stages of development, he cannot detoxify chemicals efficiently. For that matter, it is extremely important to pay attention to the well-being of pregnant women; fumes inhaled by the mother can pass through the placenta.

Although we are focusing on the nursery, use the same precautions in other rooms in the house that you may consider refurbishing with fresh paint or new carpets, drapes, or furniture. Wherever the baby or the mom-to-be will breathe, off-gassing chemicals can be harmful.

So when is the best time to apply fresh paint or install new carpet or furniture? Ideally it is before you even start a family. I realize this may not be possible, and in such cases, it is necessary to take precautions. A pregnant mom should not paint or be involved with any designing project that will potentially expose her to toxins. She should avoid any recently painted room until the fumes have completely disappeared. If a painting project in the nursery begins or continues after the baby is at home, keep her in your bedroom for a few weeks in a safety-approved crib or bassinet so she won't be inhaling air pollutants.

Keep the freshly painted nursery well ventilated—with windows opened and fans turned on to push the fumes out and bring fresh air in. Do this until you can no longer detect any odor. It's best to perform these projects during the summer months when it is warm enough to keep windows open and fans on. (In hot climates, the best time may be during cooler months, when the air conditioner is not on.)

Remember that if your home was built before 1978, you should test your home for lead paint, especially before remodeling or renovating. (See the section on lead in this chapter, above.)

Air out a room as long as possible, optimally for at least several days to a few weeks. Don't allow your child in the room while it is being painted and wait until the fumes have completely disappeared before letting your baby or child sleep in the room.

Select and Use Paint Carefully

Many paints contain VOCs, which do not stay in the paint. As the paint dries and evaporates, the VOCs are released into the air. To minimize your child's exposure, select water-based latex paints, which generally have fewer VOCs than oil-based paints. Also look for low-VOC paints, which are specially formulated to be low in polluting emissions. There are also VOC-free or No-VOC paints, which do not emit any fumes. If there is no information available on the paint can label, request the materials safety data sheet from the manufacturer or paint store. Even if you use the lower VOC paints, make sure the newly painted room is ventilated well. Children and pregnant women should stay out of the area until the paint is dry and the odor is gone.

Use Area Rugs over a Floor of Wood, Cork Tiles, Bamboo, or Natural Linoleum

New carpets emit VOCs from the fabric treatment (fire-resistant products or stain guard), glued backing, and adhesives. Infants and small children are especially vulnerable, since they are closer to the floor and spend much of their time on the floor. Moreover, all carpets—no matter what their age—can trap dust, mold, lead, and tracked-in pesticide. You've probably never thought about the significance of the floor, but when choosing, why not consider flooring such as wooden floors, cork tiles, bamboo, or natural linoleum; these are all preferable to fitted carpets.

You can provide a softer cover by using washable area rugs and positioning them over nonslip mats. If you're planning to use synthetic carpet, ask the sales person to allow your new carpet to ventilate for several days before bringing it to your home. When the installer arrives, have him either tack the carpet down or use low-VOC adhesives. When cleaning the floor or carpet, use mild cleaners instead of detergents containing solvents.

Look for Furniture Made of Solid Wood or Formaldehyde-Free Products

Formaldehyde can be emitted from some new products such as laminated wood, pressed wood, and particle board because of the glue in the products. Look for furniture made of solid wood or formaldehyde-free particle and fiber board, or use a low-toxic sealant to reduce formaldehyde seepage. Prior to installation or delivery, request that manufacturers or suppliers air out products in their warehouse—with all coverings or packaging removed—or do it at your home for a few weeks, either outdoors on a porch or in a well-ventilated, unoccupied area, such as a shed or garage.

Review and Safety Checklist

✓ If your home was built before 1978, have it professionally tested for lead, especially if you plan to remodel or renovate. If lead paint must be removed, hire a certified lead-abatement contractor.

✓ Test the tap water in your home for lead, especially if you have an older home.

✓ Use cold water for drinking and cooking.

✓ Be aware of products in your home that may contain lead, and investigate lead hazards in other places your child frequents.

✓ Seal or replace pressure-treated wood around your home.

✓ Do not allow your child to play in spaces tainted by seepage from pressure-treated wood.

✓ Test for radon in the air with a home test kit. If there is radon in the air, investigate your water by contacting your utility company or, if your water comes from a private well, contact a certified lab to do the test.

✓ Fix your home if your radon level is confirmed to be 4 picoCuries per liter (pCi/L) or higher. Hire a qualified radon mitigation contractor.

✓ Perform regular maintenance and inspection on all fuel-burning appliances and repair any leaks immediately. Unless you are an experienced installer, hire a professional to install fuel-burning appliances.

✓ Never run a car in a garage or use charcoal or a portable generator indoors. Keep all gas appliances properly vented.

✓ Teach your child the difference between the sound of the carbon monoxide detector and that of the smoke alarm.

✓ Don't smoke around children, and don't let anyone else smoke around them. Don't smoke if you are pregnant. Be a role model to your children by not smoking in front of them. Even better quit altogether; keep yourself healthy for your child.

✓ Deprive pests of food and water.

✓ Keep all pesticides locked away, out of sight. Keep all such products in their original container, clearly labeled.

✓ Get rid of pests by eliminating their hiding places, plugging their entries, and, when possible, using less toxic methods to destroy them. Use integrated pest management.

✓ If you are pregnant, do not paint or become involved in any project that may expose you to toxins. Complete tasks well ahead of the baby's arrival so he won't be inhaling air pollutants.

✓ Select paint carefully and look for furniture made of solid wood or formaldehyde-free products.

✓ For the nursery floor, use wood, cork tile, bamboo, or natural linoleum. Washable area rugs are safer than carpeting.

The Home Office

One of the advantages of the home office is that it makes a parent available to the children all day long. One of the disadvantages of the home office is that it makes a parent available to the children all day long. Okay, so it's a mixed blessing, but it is likely that one reason for your having a home office is that it allows you to care for your child. If you must use hazardous materials in your work, safety measures for a home office can be a little tricky. Separating the office from the rest of the house and keeping children out could defeat one of the main reasons for its being there.

An office in which only adults are present is vastly different from a child-friendly office. Naturally if there are hazardous materials that are part of the business or the tasks at hand, children must be kept out, regardless of the parent's desire for availability. For most home offices, however, this is not an issue. Nonetheless, materials that are not intrinsically hazardous can make a home office a minefield of danger to children.

If you are a dedicated do-it-yourselfer, you could probably write some of this chapter yourself, especially after reading the previous chapters. For the sake of brevity, we'll try not to be overly repetitious. Let's consider safety measures having to do with items specifically found in the home office.

Using Care with Furniture and Office Equipment

Prevent Furniture from Tipping Over

Secure all bookcases, file cabinets, and tall wall furniture to the walls with angle braces or anchors. You're more likely to have cords snaking across the floor in an office than in other rooms of the house, so take care to secure all loose cords to prevent tripping. This is as important for Mom and Dad as for Baby, but in addition to tripping, a child could drag office equipment down on himself. It's amazing the amount of weight a small body—especially a falling one—can move, and you probably have some pretty heavy stuff in your office.

Prevent Poisoning

The same houseplants found elsewhere in the house might be found here, too. Nothing new there. In addition to household cleaners found in other rooms, however, there is an array of other poisonous substances unique to the home office, such as special cleaners, toners, correction fluids, inks (including markers), and rubber cement. The solution is twofold: keep such supplies in a locked cabinet and always put items away in that cabinet after every use.

Prevent Choking, Suffocation, Strangulation, and Entrapment

Talk about land mines! Staples, paper clips, pens, pencils, thumbtacks—even the caps for pens and markers should be kept out of reach of little hands (and mouths). Keep such items in a locked drawer. This may seem to be a lot of trouble—a colossal inconvenience—but remember the reason: that little bundle of energy who keeps disrupting your concentration as you try to work is more precious than a convenient paper clip. (That's why you're at home!)

Keep waste cans in which you toss anything but paper tightly covered, and avoid storage chests. If you must have a chest, use the same guidelines offered in Chapter 1, "Creating a Safe Nursery"; while you're focusing on business, your child may look at the chest and think she's discovered a cozy place to hide or curl up for a nap. Window blind cords are just as dangerous in the office as they are in the rest of the house. Take necessary steps to safeguard your child.

Prevent Electrocution, Burns, and Fires

Here, too, you should protect all open electrical outlets with outlet covers. The temptation to overload electrical circuits and overuse extension cords may be greater in the office than elsewhere.

For the safety of the entire household, resist the temptation. If you need to use an extension cord, be sure to use one that is rated for the amount of watts that will be consumed by the devices you are using. (Add up all the wattage used by each piece of equipment and make sure the total is less than the capacity of the extension cord.)

Consider using surge protectors that have built-in sensors to detect a short or an overload that could start a fire. Also consider an extension cord or wall adapter that provides GFCI (ground fault circuit interrupter) protection similar to what is now standard for outlets in bathrooms and kitchens. Get covers for all the power strips and surge protectors in your office. These plastic covers are like tunnels that encase the power strip. There is an opening at the top for cords of all sizes to come through, and on some cord covers, a latching door enabling you to access the on-off switch without taking off the entire cover. Once in place these covers are a challenge for even adults to open. Just keep in mind that nothing is entirely childproof.

You desire a child-friendly office, so you want your child to be able to play there. When he's still in a playpen, that's no problem, but when he starts crawling look out! He'll want to play under desks and tables, and you don't want to say no to everything. However, a desk or table that has electric wires under it offers no safe space for a child.

As in the kitchen, hot beverages should be kept away from the edge of a desk or table. Use a spill-resistant mug, just as you would if you carried your coffee to work on a long commute. To maximize the probability that your child stays out of harm's way in your office, designate a safe area in a corner as her play area, or use a playpen. Remember to take frequent breaks so she can leave the playpen or play area and move around under her own steam in a safe environment. These periods will aid her development and, you may discover, enhance your own productivity.

Guard against your child's spilling liquids on such equipment as your computer, monitor, or printer. To be on the safe side, turn off these devices when they are not in use, and cover monitors, keyboards, towers, and printers. This is especially important if you get caught up in multitasking—easy to do at home.

Prevent Bumps, Cuts, and Scrapes

You'll want to minimize sharp corners in your office, just as you do in the rest of the house. Corner and edge bumpers might reduce a busy parent's nasty bruises as well as prevent cuts and scrapes for the child. Sharp implements such as scissors, staplers, letter openers, and paper shredders should be kept in locked drawers and cabinets.

Get Real

All right. You know your child. You know your work habits. As you were reading the above cautions, did you have an increasing sense of impending doom . . . or, at least, a feeling that all this is simply impossible? In that case, maybe it is. If your child, right now, in this stage of her life, cannot be safe in your home office, you must consider hiring a babysitter. (See Chapter 13, "Hiring a Babysitter or Choosing a Day Care Facility.")

As long as the baby is in a playpen, keeping dangerous items away from her is possible. A child who listens and usually obeys can be given her own space in the office with books, paper, crayons, and a small basket of toys on hand. However, it is likely that there will be a period that comes between those two ages when the office is simply too dangerous for her presence. You'll know when that time comes. To know when it passes, do a trial run every so often. Let her become an "employee," with a specific job such as drawing pictures to decorate the walls. Please! Not on the walls!

If you have employees other than that charming child busily coloring on the floor—the one trying hard not to color the carpet as well—make sure they take the same precautions you take for the safety of your child.

Review and Safety Checklist

- ✓ Prevent injuries by securing all bookcases, file cabinets, and tall furniture to the wall.

- ✓ Keep poisonous office supplies in a locked cabinet and always put items away after use.

✓ Keep small office items such as paper clips, tacks, and pen caps in a locked drawer when not in use. Keep waste cans tightly covered and avoid storage chests with lids.

✓ Don't overload circuits, use a surge protector, and keep your child away from electrical wires. Turn off electrical appliances when they are not in use.

✓ Minimize sharp corners: use corner- and edge-bumpers.

Hiring a Babysitter or Choosing a Day Care Facility

You will never have a more important—or more rewarding—responsibility than caring for your child. When you first hold that tiny hand, your heart will tell you that you want to be with your child every moment. Nonetheless, you cannot do it alone. Regardless of whether you have extended family nearby, day care services and babysitters can be invaluable as you seek to give your child the best possible care. The search for quality care must begin as soon as possible. You can't put off till the last minute the pursuit of a good babysitter, and some day care facilities may have up to an 18-month waiting list.

In-home babysitters are not subject to state licensing. That's why it is so important that you thoroughly interview, screen, and manage your child's sitter. Trust both your head and your feelings. If your gut says there is something wrong, do not hire this person to watch your child. On the other hand, if your feeling is that this person would be a good caregiver for your child, go a little further in your investigation.

Day care centers range from small independent companies to church-run establishments and large national chains. Some companies, for the convenience of their employees, have day care centers in their office complex. Whatever the size and type, the best day care center is one that caters to the needs of both the parents and the children. Don't be fooled by promotion. Ascertain whether a center implements the kind of care it promotes and check to be sure it provides loving and respectful child care.

The way day care centers operate and the facilities they are required to have are governed by state regulations. All states have minimum licensing regulations for child care programs that include health, safety, and sanitation. However, a state license is not a guarantee of high quality. States vary in terms of how stringent the minimum requirements are. You can contact your state's child care licensing agency to find out what rules and regulations it requires. Inquire there to discover if there are any substantiated complaints against the facilities you are investigating.

A facility accredited by the National Association for the Education of Young Children should go to the top of your list, and getting that information has never been easier. The association has an online database (see Appendix E, "Helpful Resources") listing day care centers that measure up to the organization's standards. Be aware, however, that some good day care centers may not show up on this list. The accreditation procedure is expensive and time-consuming, and some excellent facilities may not have the time, the staff, or the money to acquire the association's accreditation. In the section on judging a day care facility, you'll learn what to consider as you review facility, staff, and references.

Finding the Right Sitter

If you need a sitter on an occasional basis only—let's say, for a romantic dinner out with your spouse—use a trusted family member or ask a reliable friend who has a young child to consider watching your baby with his or hers for a few hours. You will return the favor at another time during the week. While this is a solution for special occasions, for many families, having a regular babysitter is a must. Finding the right person for the job is one of the most important tasks you have.

Getting Started

Ask Around or Hire an Agency

At first, you may feel more comfortable recruiting caring family, friends, and neighbors whom you know well. That's certainly a good place to start, especially when your child is an infant or toddler. When you must go outside that circle, draw on it by getting recommendations from friends, relatives, neighbors, doctors, clerics, or local organizations such as the YMCA. If they have no advice or if the pickings seem slim, consider using a reputable babysitter service. The company will prescreen the sitters they send to you.

In addition to having interviewed any nanny or babysitter sent you for approval, a babysitting service also should have required the completion of an extensive application and done a thorough background check—from employment references to possible criminal history. However, you should not take this for granted. Ask to see the employment application. Inquire about the thoroughness of the background check. Investigate the company first, then double-check the candidate's references. A call to the Better Business Bureau will tell you if there have been complaints registered against the company.

Consider Age

A service will usually employ older individuals. If the choice is do-it-yourself all the way, make sure the sitter is at least 13 years old. A good starting age for babysitting is around 15 or 16. Before hiring a teenager, talk to her parents. When it comes down to it, however, you must interview the candidates and make a judgment about the fit between the potential employee and your child.

Conducting the Interview

Evaluate the Candidate's Attributes

The key attributes to look for are maturity, trustworthiness, experience, and responsibility. You can ask general questions to give you insight into the potential sitter's personality. What are her goals? Interests? What does he do for fun? The specific answers may not be as important as the way in which they are answered. Certainly, it is better to select someone who already has babysitting experience and a good reputation. If a candidate cites experience, get names and phone numbers and tell her you are going to call past employers. Check references thoroughly.

Know How the Candidate Will Handle Discipline

An important element of your interview is to ask how the candidate handles discipline. No one should hit a child for any reason. Try to ask this question in an open way so that you will get an honest answer.

See How the Candidate Interacts With Your Child

At some time during the interview, it might be helpful to see how the potential sitter interacts with your child. Keep in mind the personality of your child, however. If he is very shy and takes a while to open up with strangers, you can't expect the sitter to make an immediate connection. On the other hand, the sitter's response to your child's personality may be informative.

Following Up When a Candidate Seems Promising

Check References

This point has already been made, but it cannot be emphasized enough. Ask for references from past employers, teachers, counselors, relatives, friends, neighbors, and anyone else you or the candidate can think of. When you speak to them, ask if they are aware of any other places the individual has worked—an invaluable source if the applicant has left out any information.

Investigate the Candidate's Background

When you think you have found the right person for the job, you may want to consider doing a criminal background check. Let's face it, this person will be performing the most important job in the world—taking care of your baby! Let the candidate know beforehand that you will be performing a criminal background check as part of the evaluation process. Procedures vary from state to state on how to obtain this information. Check with your local law enforcement agency, and they can refer you to the proper authority. There is also a variety of resources on the internet that can perform these services. You should also contact your local Department of Social Services, which maintains reports of child care abuse or neglect in your community. Ask if the candidate has ever had a report of misconduct filed against her and if so, learn the outcome of that report.

Find Out about the Candidate's Health

Learn about the potential sitter's health. Ask if she has had a recent medical exam. If she has not, you can offer to pay for one. With so many communicable diseases—old ones like tuberculosis and new ones like SARS (sudden acute respiratory syndrome)—you cannot be too careful.

Ask about the Candidate's Training

Be certain the sitter is trained in infant/child CPR and first aid. If you like a potential sitter who has not had such training, recommend that she take a babysitter training course at a local hospital or safety organization (such as the Red Cross).

If you must use an inexperienced babysitter, have her begin with gradual responsibilities—watching the baby while you are at home or sitting while you are away for a brief period, half an hour, perhaps. Even if a sitter has had experience, I recommend that you have trial days (with pay) before offering the job on a permanent basis.

If the Candidate Will Be Transporting Your Child, Check the Driving Record

If the sitter will be driving with your baby, it is important to check her driving record. If she has had a DUI or speeding tickets, you do not want her to drive with your child in the car. Contact your state's motor vehicle bureau to obtain a copy of her report. Many states now require the sitter's authorization to release this information. Once the sitter's driving record checks out fine, make sure she knows how to use and correctly install the baby's car seat.

Setting Guidelines

Give the Sitter a Tour of Your Home

As you show the sitter your home, point out and demonstrate how to use all the safety devices you have installed (gates, child-resistant latches, and locks). Show her where you store supplies, such as a flashlight, first aid kit, and fire extinguisher. Identify those areas of your home that are off-limits to your children (and the sitter). Familiarize her with your fire escape plan. Give her this book to read.

Be specific about your expectations and what information is important for the sitter to know. Write these down and discuss them, too. If your child has special medical needs or takes medicine the sitter may need to administer, explain the dosage and point to where you have written down that information. Be sure the sitter understands that she should never give the child any medicine without your permission and instructions. Tell her about specific foods the child eats or shouldn't eat. Also, be careful when explaining the child's bedtime or naptime. If there is a favorite bedtime ritual, your sitter needs to know what it is. What TV shows or videos may your child watch? What books may she read? Does she have a favorite toy? Where is it?

Point Out the Don'ts of Activities with Your Child

Tell the sitter she should never bathe your baby or take him swimming. These activities are high risk and unnecessary. The babysitter should never take your child away from your home while you are gone without your knowledge and consent.

Explain What Is Expected Of the Sitter

Make sure your sitter understands the rules governing her conduct before she takes the job: no friends allowed, no cooking, no smoking in the house. Be explicit about phone calls, too. The sitter should keep personal phone calls to a minimum; however, stress that she should never hesitate to call or beep you for any questions. I always explained that no matter how minor or silly it might appear, I would always welcome the call. Stress that you do not want her to leave your child alone for one second. You expect her to be as vigilant as you are when you are at home.

Devise an Emergency Plan

Arrange for a neighbor to be available if there is a problem. This should be someone who is trusted by the family and who is almost always at home. Be sure the specified person has met the babysitter. Point out the emergency information posted by the telephone. (See Chapter 14, "Preparing for Emergencies," for emergency numbers that should be posted.)

Be Concise with Parting Instructions

It won't hurt to have these last-minute instructions written down along with the other guidelines:

- keep the doors and windows locked

- don't let anyone, even a friend, into the house without permission

- know the emergency plan.

Finally, as you go, reiterate, "Don't hesitate to call me."

Checking Up

Be Observant While You Are at Home—Check Up During and After Your Absence

Before you leave, give your sitter a chance to interact with your child. This can be going on while you give last-minute instructions. Observe their interaction. During your absence, especially when the sitter is still new to you, check in to see how things are going. After the sitter has left, ask your child how she feels about the sitter.

How to Judge Day Care Facilities

After investigating the licensing of the centers on your list, you will focus on location. If at all possible, you'll want to be able to drop off and pick up your child at a place that is close to the route between home and work for at least one parent. Next, find out how long each center has been in business. Not only are older establishments more likely to be stable, they are also more likely to provide a broad range of references. Find out how much each center charges for child care. If a facility's fees are beyond the limits of your budget, you will not want to spin your wheels checking it out. Now ask around. What do other parents say about the centers on your list? Listen primarily to parents who agree with you about the importance of safety and any other policies you deem significant.

If you live in an area where the choices are so narrow you'd run out of centers if you used all the above criteria, this is going to be even more of a do-it-yourself project. Whether you have a short list of 10 or 1, there are steps you can take to find the center that is most likely to keep your baby safe.

The first time you visit the center, make an appointment so you can meet with the director. Not only will you be able to determine the philosophy of the center from the person in charge, but you will also avoid taking a staff person away from his job. (This is also a good time to ask about insurance coverage.) After the initial visit, drop by unannounced a couple of times, at different times of the day. Are the rooms well ventilated and filled with light and joy? Would you want to come to a place like this on a regular basis? If you wouldn't like it, your child probably wouldn't either.

Going After Hard Facts

Find Out About Employees and the Ratio of Children to Caregivers

Look for a child care program that has a low child-teacher ratio. The ratios are important as a way to assess how much individual attention your child will get. The younger your child, the more important this is. In addition to low child-teacher ratios, the overall size of the program is important. Each state sets a minimum requirement according to the age of the child. Below is the ideal ratio standard of child to caregiver, along with the ideal maximum number of children in the group.

Age	Ideal Child / Caregiver Ratio	Ideal Maximum Group Size
birth-12 months	3:1	6
13-30 months	4:1	8
31-35 months	5:1	10
3-year-olds	7:1	14
4-year-olds	8:1	16

(Source: American Academy of Pediatrics, American Public Health Association and National Resource Center for Health and Safety in Child Care. Caring for Our Children: National Health and Safety Performance Standards: Guidelines for Out-of-Home Child Care Programs, 2nd edition. Elk Grove Village, IL: American Academy of Pediatrics, 2002.)

Find Out about Hiring Policies

Ask: What is the rate of employee turnover? The answer to this question will tell you if your child will be able to rely on his caregiver's being there for him. It may also indicate possible management problems. What are the requirements for those who are employed to work with the children? NAEYC recommends that early childhood teachers (staff who are responsible for the care and education of a group of children from birth through age 5) have at least a CDA Credential or an associate degree in Early Childhood Education/Child Development or the equivalent. Early Childhood Teacher Assistants should have been trained in Early Childhood Education/Child Development or participate in ongoing professional development programs.

Have all staff and caregivers submitted to background and criminal checks? What kinds of training and certification are required? Has the staff been trained in infant/child CPR and first aid? You'll want your day care center to be as careful as you are when you choose a babysitter. There should be at least one staff person present at all times who is trained in the Heimlich maneuver and CPR for infants and children.

Your child's health will be affected by the health of his caregivers. Ask: Is the health of employees a matter of concern for the center? Are employees required to have a complete medical check up? What is the policy when an employee is sick? Do any employees smoke? If so, is there a place for them to do so outside the air-circulation system in the building?

Ask Questions about Holidays, Schedule Flexibility, and Fines

Ask about holiday schedules as well as regular daily hours. What days is the center closed? Find out ahead of time how flexible the drop-off and pick-up times may be. Learn what happens when a parent is late to pick up a child. Most centers charge extra fees if you are late. Find out if a center can make an arrangement regarding charges, especially if your work schedule does not match the center's usual hours. It is important to work this out ahead of time rather than rushing around with your child to get there, rushing from work to pick up the child, missing the deadline day after day, and always paying fines for lateness.

Looking at Intangibles

Ask about Programs and Policies

Ask about discipline and ask to see the written policies regarding it. Punishment administered by center staff should never involve grabbing or hitting and should be no more than a brief time-out from play activities.

Health issues are matters of policy, too. One issue you might not consider is whether babies are separated from toddlers. This is important to the health of both age groups. Find out if caregivers are required to wash their hands often, especially after changing or before feeding infants, and before snack time for older children. Are good health practices encouraged? Do caregivers make sure children wash their hands each time they use the bathroom and before snack time?

Learn how the center deals with sick children. The center should be able to provide you, in writing, the procedures followed when a child is ill or injured. There should also be information about when a parent is required to keep a sick child at home. It is important, as well, that the center have a good filing system, a place where emergency contact information on each child is kept, along with a list of your child's allergies and medical needs. Ask what procedure is used to make sure these needs are heeded.

Even infants should be engaged rather than left alone in a crib or playpen. Ask: What kinds of activities are provided, and what is the educational philosophy behind them? How large a role does television play in activities at the center? Are children taken outside each day? What will your child be doing each day? How is the child's progress evaluated? Try to find a center with a philosophy close to yours. It is important for you to figure out exactly what you expect of the facility so that you will know what questions to ask in this regard. How the center observes religious holidays may be of concern to you. If so, ask about the policy.

Are strict rules followed regarding who can pick up your child from the facility? There should be a signed form kept on file indicating those individuals who are authorized to pick up each child. A driver's license or photo ID should be checked before the child is released.

Learn What the Center Expects of Parents

Some day care centers require parents to provide occasional—or regular—hands-on assistance with the children. You will want to ask about the other parents who comply with this requirement. Are they supervised? What are their backgrounds? If there is such a requirement, learn the extent of necessary participation and decide whether it is something you wish to do.

Is a parent required to bring food for the child or are snacks and meals furnished? Are the meals and snacks provided by the center age appropriate, varied, and nutritious? How large a supply of diapers should be brought, and should they be brought daily or weekly? Are other supplies furnished?

Are parents encouraged to communicate with the center and with individual caregivers? What are the acceptable ways to do this? Especially with infants and toddlers, there should be daily communication between parent and caregiver. Is there a place where nursing moms may come to breast-feed? May parents visit?

May they drop in unannounced? Never put your child in a day care facility that does not have an open-door policy or requires you to call first.

Observe the Day Care Center

So far you've just asked questions. Now request a tour of the facility at a time when caregivers and children are going about their routine. Keep these questions in mind:

Is it safe? The criteria to help you make this judgment are in every chapter in this book. Look for smoke alarms and fire extinguishers. If you don't see them, ask where they are. Are there dangling cords of any kind? Are there safety covers on electrical outlets? Do windows have safety features? Are there adequate fire exits? Are periodic fire drills conducted at the center? Has the facility been childproofed the way you have childproofed your home?

Is it clean? If it's unsanitary it isn't safe, but this is not a matter of squeaky-clean neatness. On the one hand, there should be orderliness, but if everything is put away and in its place when children are around, it is a sad place for a child to be. On the other hand, you'll want to know if soiled diapers are disposed of in a sealed plastic-lined container out of the reach of children. Is there a separate area for changing diapers, and is the diaper-changing area sanitized after each child has been changed? Is there a separate area for preparing food? Are the kitchen and bathroom surfaces routinely cleaned and disinfected? Ask where the children sleep or rest, and make sure that area is especially clean.

Are toys and equipment age-appropriate and in good condition? Are they cleaned and disinfected routinely? There should be an outside, enclosed play area. Look it over and make sure the facility follows the safety precautions described in Chapter 6, "Safety in the Backyard."

Do the caregivers and children appear happy? Do they seem healthy? Watch how the caregivers interact with children. Do the caregivers get down to eye-level with the child? Are crying babies attended immediately? How do staff members calm a crying child?

Some additional matters to observe or inquire about: Is there a separate crib for each infant? Are current SIDS recommendations followed? Are infants held individually for feeding? How frequently are the children taken to the toilet or diapered? Are first aid kits handy? Ask to see them, and check the contents against the checklist in the following chapter.

Check References

It does no good to ask for references and not check them. Look over the previous five items to help you know what to ask. If a child no longer attends that day care center, ask the parent why.

Following Up after Your Child Is Enrolled

Pay Attention to Your Child

If your child cries every time you bring her to the center, find out why. Once a toddler can talk, ask about the personnel by name, and watch her reaction. Your child's general mood is important. If she is always sad or upset when she is picked up at day care (other than insisting she wants to stay a little longer!), find out why.

After enrolling your child in a program, if you learn that food, rest, or bathroom privileges are withheld as punishment, report the facility to your state's child care licensing agency. And find another center for your child.

Review and Safety Checklist

- ✓ Choose a sitter based on age and personal attributes such as attitude, apparent maturity, and interaction with your child.

- ✓ Find out how the sitter views discipline.

- ✓ Investigate a potential sitter's background, health, training and driving record (if the sitter will be transporting your child).

- ✓ Explain the house rules and devise an emergency plan with the sitter

- ✓ Give clear parting instructions—perhaps written as well as spoken—and stress that the sitter may call or beep you with any questions.

- ✓ Check up on the sitter during and after the engagement.

✓ When making a list of child care centers to review, first check to see which ones are accredited by the National Association for the Education of Young Children, then call your state's child care licensing agency to inquire about the facilities.

✓ If possible, narrow down the list to include mainly facilities close to your home-to-work route. Ask other parents what they know about the centers remaining on your list.

✓ Interview the director. Ask about employees (their backgrounds and training), payment plans, schedules (hours and days), policies, programs, and procedures.

✓ Learn what is expected of you, as a parent, and find out what you will be required to furnish for your child.

✓ Find out how parents may communicate about their child with caregivers and ask about the visitation policy.

✓ Observe the day care center for safety, cleanliness, and demeanor of caregivers and children as they interact.

✓ Check references and ask questions about all issues that concern you; verify what you have observed or been told.

Preparing for Emergencies

Y ou've been through the entire house, yard, and office, getting rid of hazards—locking, bracing, covering, and planning. But emergencies happen. No matter what area of your life you think you have planned to the nth degree, events occur that are not expected and not happy. There are steps you can take to be ready. Some are as simple as writing down names and numbers on a form and keeping copies of the completed form handy by your telephones and in your car. Others are nearly as simple—a matter of gathering together supplies you hope will never be needed and making plans you hope you'll never have to follow. In like manner, there is something you should know how to do: CPR. All parents and caregivers should take an infant/child CPR and first aid course. It is a good idea for parents to carry the following with them whenever they leave the house: a fully charged cell phone, and on their key chain, a flashlight and whistle, which can be used to signal for help.

Although you can make yourself ready, it is extremely important that your child know what to do in case of an emergency when you have become disabled or are not available for some reason. Start teaching your youngest children the simplest information: the first digits of your address, the name of your street, and the color of your house. The ultimate goal is for your toddler to memorize her first and last name, her complete address (including city and state) and your phone number, including area code. Practice with her the concept of what constitutes an emergency and practice till you are sure she knows how to dial 9-1-1 or 0 in case you have an emergency that incapacitates you when you are alone with your child.

The responsibility for making sure you have the appropriate supplies on hand rests with you. Below you will find lists of items that belong in your home's first aid kit and disaster supplies kit, which will help you prepare for a wide range of emergencies in your home. All medicines should be kept in child-resistant packaging. Store kits locked out of the sight and reach of children but easily accessible to adults. Remember: When giving medicine to children, always check with the pediatrician first. Use the measuring dispenser that comes packaged with the child's medication.

One of the items in the first aid kit with which you may not be familiar is electrolyte solution. It is given to small children to prevent dehydration from illness, vomiting, and diarrhea.

First Aid Kit

- First aid manual

- Non-latex gloves

- Sterile adhesive bandages in a variety of sizes

- Sterile gauze pads and rolls

- Hypoallergenic adhesive tape

- Cotton-tipped swabs

- Absorbent cotton

- Antiseptic wipes

- Soap

- Antiseptic cream (for example, bacitracin)

- Antiseptic solution (for example, hydrogen peroxide)

- Hydrocortisone cream

- Calamine lotion

- Tweezers

- Sharp scissors

- Digital thermometer (Do not use glass mercury thermometers because of the dangers of mercury exposure and broken glass.)

- Petroleum jelly

- Disposable instant ice bags

- Acetaminophen

- Electrolyte solution (for example, Pedialyte)

Call your local poison control center at 1-800-222-1222 to ask what emergency products (such as activated charcoal) they advise you to keep at home. You'll want to have the recommended product(s) on hand if you need them. Always call the poison center first, before treating a poisoning.

Preparing for Disaster

The need for having a disaster supplies kit is not new. People have kept them for centuries in preparation for storms of various kinds and other natural disasters. In wartime, too, having a disaster supplies kit has always been prudent. Today all of us are aware of dangers we might face as we go about our daily lives. Your children are aware, on some level, that we live in a dangerous world. You can use the assembly of a disaster supplies kit as a way of talking about the remoteness of the possibility of disaster and giving assurances that your family is taking steps to ensure safety no matter what happens.

Select a room in your home that will be your safe room. A big closet or interior room would be ideal. A hallway or bathroom will serve as well. If there are windows in the safe room, you may actually get a chance to use that duct tape you've heard so much about, but only if advised by local officials to "shelter-in-place" for a chemical emergency—not for other purposes. Try to use a room with no outside walls or only one outside wall, and small, if any, windows.

Store the first aid and disaster supplies kit near, or as close as possible, to the exit door (such as in an entry hall closet). This will enable you to grab it and go in case you need to leave and will save time in an emergency. When a disaster happens and you decide to use your safe room, you can take your kits there. Let everyone in the family know where the kits are stored.

It is best to arrange to have a hard-wired telephone in the safe room that you will be using. Regular phones that plug into a standard phone jack get their power from the phone company (which has emergency generators to power the telephone network), not from the power in your home. So if the power goes out, the phone will probably still work. Portable phones and cell phones are not reliable during a power outage and after major disasters.

If your child is old enough to express personal safety concerns, she is old enough to make suggestions about what to include with the disaster supplies. Food, water, and batteries should be replaced periodically with new items. You might have a disaster drill, with the family gathering in the safe room and staying for an hour, eating some of the stored food and drinking some of the water. Be sure to immediately replace everything that was consumed. This is a good time to check use by dates. If food items are close to expiration, why not donate them to local food banks so they can be used right away? Replace them immediately.

An important item worth investing in is a battery-powered NOAA weather radio. (A National Oceanic and Atmospheric Administration radio broadcasts national weather service warnings, forecasts, and other hazard information 24 hours a day.)

Your kit should contain, at a minimum, a 3-day supply. Keep items in easy-to-carry containers like duffle bags, backpacks, or covered trash receptacles. Plan to use only battery-powered lights, never candles. Begin with the basic list below and add details as a family.

Disaster Supplies Kit

- Baby supplies (for example, formula, jars of baby food, diapers, and moist towelettes)

- Toys and activities for the children

- Supply of essential medications (Check with your physician or pharmacist about how best to store.)

- Books for the adults

- Flashlight
- Battery-operated portable radio (preferably NOAA weather radio)
- Extra batteries of appropriate size
- Duct tape
- Plastic sheeting
- Blankets
- Canned food and can opener
- Bottled water (1 gallon per day per person)
- Paper cups, plates, plastic utensils
- Cash or traveler's checks and change
- Personal identification
- Extra set of keys
- Extra set of clothes
- Important family documents, stored in a fire- and water-proof container
- Plastic garbage bags and ties
- Toilet paper
- Essential items for your pets
- Wrench or pliers, in case you need to turn off utilities

Emergency Plans When Away from Home

You and your family may not be together when an emergency situation occurs. A storm could hit, or your power grid could go out. If your child attends day care, find out if the center has a disaster plan. Ask where caregivers would take the children in the event of an emergency and know what supplies the center provides. Both spouses should be familiar with each other's workplace evacuation plans and what supplies they provide. Decide which one of you would pick up your child if necessary. Establish a meeting place for all the family members.

Go a step further and designate an out-of-town family member or friend who will serve as the call center for your family. If any member cannot contact another, the out-of-town "control" can relay information. If there is an emergency situation over a broad area, you'll have a better chance of communicating with a long-distance call than a local one.

Because someone else may need to make calls for you, list the out-of-town contact at the day care center and at both parents' workplace. For each family member, create an emergency backpack containing the special items that person needs. For example, for an adult, include:

- a three-day supply of prescription medicine

- any necessary food supplements or OTC medication

- a paperback book in his favorite genre

- a small flashlight with extra batteries

- bottled water and nonperishable food.

For a child:

- if she uses prescription or over the counter medications, make sure that her daycare or school has a supply to be able to give to her as prescribed. Do not allow children to keep prescription or OTC medications with them in their own personal belongings.

- a comfort toy

- a 1-day supply of baby's needs

If possible, leave the appropriate backpacks where each family member is most likely to be when not at home—at work or at the day care center. (Be sure to rotate prescription medication often.)

Always keep important information on hand:

- A current photograph of your child should stay with you. This is the single most important tool for recovering a missing child. It's a good idea to replace the photo every 6 months with an up-to-date color photograph.

- Other important data to have available: your child's most recent dental and medical records, a videotape of the child, a complete description of the child, fingerprints, and a DNA kit.

Form for Emergency Numbers

Use this form to collect all emergency numbers for use in your home. In a crisis situation, it should be handy for you or anyone staying in your home to use. Post a copy near every telephone. Post one in the safe room, as well.

Emergency __*911* or *0*_____

Police _____

Fire Department _____

Ambulance _____

Pediatrician _____

Family doctor _____

Dentist _____

Poison Control Hotline __1-*800-222-1222*_____

Pharmacy _____

Out-of-town family contact_____

Information to Give in Emergencies

Home address (include all cross streets so that directions can be given):

_____

_____

Home phone number _____

Personal information about the child:

Child's name_____

Date of birth _____

Weight _____

Allergies _____

Current medications _____

Medical conditions _____

How to reach family members (include beeper and cellular phone numbers):

Mom's work numbers _____

Dad's work numbers _____

Nearest relative or neighbor_____

Phone number_____

Review and Safety Checklist

✓ Assemble a first aid and disaster supplies kit. Store kits near the exit door. Kits should be locked out of reach of children but easily accessible to adults. Rotate supplies such as batteries, water, canned goods, and medication.

✓ Designate a safe room in your home and arrange to have a hard-wired telephone in it.

✓ If she is old enough to understand, allow your child to help assemble the disaster supplies kit and prepare the safe room.

✓ Periodically conduct a disaster drill for the entire family, staying in the safe room for a brief time and practicing any activities that might occur there.

✓ Establish a plan in the event not all family members are together. Decide upon a meeting place and who will pick up the children.

✓ Designate an out-of-town relative or friend to serve as a contact center in case family members are unable to contact each other directly.

✓ Post near every telephone a list of emergency numbers and information to give in case of emergency.

Part III

Making Special Occasions Safe

You have made your home and the places your child regularly visits as safe as possible, but you and your child don't keep to the same home routine every day of the year. There are special occasions when regular practices may fall by the wayside. Holidays present special situations and, so, require special consideration. Traveling with your baby, whether during holidays, on family vacations, or perhaps, on a trip to the mall, can be a safety nightmare if you are not prepared.

"Debra's Holiday Safety Guide" (Chapter 15) cautions you about dangers specific to various holidays and tells you how to avoid them. "Traveling with Baby" (Chapter 16) tells you everything you need to know to keep yourself and your baby safe, and to increase the probability that you will arrive at your destination with parent and baby smiling, comfortable, and glad to have made the trip.

Debra's Holiday Safety Guide

Holidays are supposed to be fun. We know that's true, but why is it that so often, something comes along to spoil the day? We won't consider here the possible psychological causes, such as having unrealistic expectations. Those are usually burdens only adults face. Adults who are parents of young children, however, have built-in happiness machines in the form of tiny faces wreathed in glowing smiles. Children come to expect what their parents can create. The expectations rest with the parents.

While I would advise parents to avoid the syndrome of beat-the-neighbors holiday plans, especially with regard to birthday parties, that decision is better left to your family and your wallet. I prefer to address safety measures that will prevent a holiday from becoming a disaster more significant than whether the paid clown appears on time to greet the guests.

Let me emphasize that the dos and don'ts discussed in this chapter are meant to help you keep the fun in the holiday, not to make you so fearful that you—and your children—are nervous wrecks. Knowing what can go wrong will help you avoid the dangers, so arm yourself with knowledge, take precautions, and enjoy!

Birthdays

The only exclusively personal holiday is one's birthday. If it happens to coincide with a more general holiday, such as the Fourth of July, Halloween, or Christmas, it may take a little additional care on the part of parents and family to make sure the birthday child does not feel cheated. However you manage it, you will still want to celebrate the big day with candles on the cake, gift wrap and ribbons, decorations, and games. Birthday candles are the exception to my safety rule that the use of real candles should be avoided around young children. That's because they are put out nearly as quickly as they are lit, and neither child nor pet would ever be left alone with candles on the cake.

If You Have a Party

Before you welcome the party guests to your home, inspect it for potential hazards from the perspective of the youngest person who will attend. Just as you crawled around to childproof your home before your baby came, now you can do it with the party in mind. Look under the sofa, move the chairs, and check all areas carefully for small objects or other hazards. Look outside, too. Remove all potential tripping hazards from your sidewalk, steps, porch, and yard. Make sure all exits in your home will remain clear.

When you decorate, do not use any small objects or sharp or breakable decorations. Because children can suffocate on deflated or broken pieces of latex balloons, avoid using them. Keep all decorations and all flammable materials away from fire and heat sources. Be equally as careful in selecting party favors. Do not allow a child to have any item that is small enough to present a choking hazard or has a small part or component that could separate during use. Read age labels to help select the safest gifts.

When choosing the menu, plan to provide a variety of healthy snacks. Do not serve hard, round food to children under 6 years old. Make sure any juice or cider to be served is pasteurized, and ask other parents beforehand if they or their children are allergic to any foods. If munchies for adults are to be served (such as peanuts or popcorn), make sure they are placed out of the sight and reach of young children.

When you buy a gift for your own child or for another birthday child, keep safety in mind. In the "Christmas or Chanukah" section below, I discuss some unsafe gifts. Safety with balloons, candles, and other decorations are also discussed in other sections of this chapter. Whether you are the host or a guest, keep an eye on discarded gift wrap, plastic bags, and ribbons. Dispose of them quickly, before a child begins to run with a ribbon around his neck. Just remember to keep children a safe distance from lit birthday cake candles. Hair and clothing may ignite when a child leans over to blow out the candles.

The Fourth of July

Our nation, too, celebrates a birthday. The Fourth of July is dear to the heart of every American, and your child will learn to love it when she gets over the trauma of the big, booming noises that hurt her ears. The youngest toddler understands birthdays, and she will appreciate this national holiday more if you explain that this is the Happy Birthday of the United States of America. Those big noises are simply side effects of the beautiful colors one sees in the night sky on this special day.

If we could stick to professional fireworks shows, our children would be much safer. Problems arise when folks decide to set off fireworks of their own. Serious burns can occur when children play with firecrackers and sparklers. Many people consider sparklers to be the ideal "safe" fireworks for the young, but these "pretty little sparkles" burn at temperatures of 2,000°F and can easily ignite clothing. Children cannot understand the danger involved and cannot act appropriately in case of emergency.

Each year thousands of fireworks-related injuries are treated in hospital emergency rooms. Because the private use of fireworks is so dangerous, I strongly recommend that you celebrate July 4th by taking your family to a professional fireworks show.

If You Decide to Use Fireworks of Your Own

In addition to following the fireworks laws in your locale, exercise extreme caution and follow the fire safety procedures noted in Chapter 8, "Fire Safety," along with these important safety tips:

- Before you do anything else, read the product instructions and warnings, and follow those guidelines.

- Fill a bucket with water and have it standing nearby—just in case.

- Before lighting fireworks, carefully check to see that children and spectators are out of range; instruct others to do the same.

- Do not allow your children to play with the fireworks and teach them to leave the area if their friends use them.

- Light fireworks on a smooth, flat surface, away from the house and away from any flammables.

- Never shoot fireworks in metal or glass containers.

- Never try to relight fireworks that have not fully functioned.

- Dispose of burned-out sparklers in a bucket of water as soon as the sparks have finished flying. Be careful, because they remain very hot.

Halloween

Gone are the days when you know your neighbors so intimately you would trust any of them with the life of your child. In these times, you cannot safely send your little ones out the door under the care of a slightly older child. Yet, because we remember fondly past Halloweens with costumes and shouts of "Trick or treat!" we try to give our children a happy holiday at the end of October.

If You Go Trick-or-Treating

I recommend skipping the practice of going door-to-door for treats, but if you or your children have your hearts set on it, there are ways to make trick-or-treating safer. First, make sure the costume is safe. How to do this is outlined in the following section, "If You Host a Party." Next, tell your child ahead of time (perhaps while you are making her costume) that you will accompany her right to the door of every house she visits. Then do it. Before you leave your house, put reflective tape on her costume and bag so she can be seen by motorists. (It won't hurt a bit if you stick strips of it on your own clothing. Your young child will love the fact that you are getting into the act. An older child will simply be embarrassed.) Equip your child with a flashlight and reflective accessories, and make sure you stay on well-lit streets.

Use the sidewalk whenever possible, and hold your child's hand when you must cross the street. Make sure your child walks from house to house; no running allowed. Tripping hazards are more abundant in the dark and on unfamiliar lawns. Running increases the risk.

Inspect all the treats your child has collected before he eats anything. Toss out any treat that is not in an original wrapper or was homemade. Also throw away any food that may pose a choking hazard for your child.

If You Host a Party

The best way to let your child have Halloween and be safe, too, is to host a Halloween party. Even at home there are hazards, but you'll be prepared by following some safety guidelines as you assemble decorations and games. The guidelines for planning a safe birthday party apply to any party with young guests, including Halloween. There are, however, some matters that you must address specifically for this October celebration. With your invitations, include a notice that there will be a costume contest and that one aspect considered in choosing winners will be safety. Let them know your own children will be dressed accordingly. Include these tips to help parents choose their children's costumes:

- Masks are great fun, but they can obstruct a child's vision and restrict breathing. I've talked my child into using makeup instead. If you can't convince your child to forego a mask he thinks is perfect, make sure he can breathe and see easily while wearing it.

- I have seen makeup that is both non-toxic and hypoallergenic at [name of a local store]. That's what I'm going to use, even though I have to use it sparingly because of my child's sensitive skin.

- I noticed when I was in [name of store] the other day that they have flame-resistant costumes; they are clearly marked. I've learned that homemade costumes can be flame resistant, too, if they are made of nylon or polyester. I won't be using candles in the jack-o-lanterns, but still, if you can, please avoid costumes made of flimsy materials; outfits with big, baggy sleeves; or apparel with billowing or long, trailing features. The costume should never be loose-fitting and 100% cotton.

- If your child's costume has accessories, please be sure they are soft and flexible. For safety's sake, we've decided not to allow any props that are hard or sharp.

- Another safety precaution I'm taking is to hem my child's costume short enough that he won't trip on it. He'll also be wearing sturdy, well-fitting shoes. If you have trouble persuading your child to dress for safety, remind him that the costume judges will consider safety above all else (including how a mask might restrict vision or breathing).

- I know you're going to drive Halloween-slow that night, but you can get your child in a party mood by letting him be a lookout for trick-or-treaters who may dart out into the road in their excitement. There will be spooks and goblins out that night!

- If we carve a jack-o-lantern, only adults will be wielding the cutting tools. I plan to let each child decorate the face of a small jack-o-lantern using non-toxic markers and paints. Your child will get to take home the jack-o-lantern he decorates. Some jack-o-lanterns may have cutouts, but you won't need a candle; a flashlight or glow stick will do beautifully.

Christmas and Chanukah

With whatever customs you celebrate this season of giving, making it a special time means making it safe, too. Candles play an important role in most of these celebrations, but my advice as a safety expert is this: Avoid using real candles around small children. Even when your children are older, it is never safe to use lit candles on a tree or near other evergreens, and no candles should ever be left unattended, especially when children of any age are in the room. Candles used properly should be in nonflammable, stable holders, in a place where they cannot be knocked down. Safer alternatives to real candles are artificial candles that either plug into an outlet or run on batteries. When you leave your home or when you go to bed during the holiday season, do not leave candles or electric decorations burning, whether they are lights on the Christmas tree or candles (even electric ones) in the window or in a menorah.

Remember, too, that some holiday plants are poisonous. These include mistletoe, holly, Christmas rose, and Jerusalem cherry. Be sure to keep these plants (and all poisonous plants) out of the reach of children. (If you suspect a poisonous plant has been ingested, contact the Poison Control Center at 1-800-222-1222.) Although the poinsettia was blamed for a death in 1919, recent studies indicate that the plant is not as highly toxic as was thought at that time. It is unlikely that ingestion of a poinsettia would be fatal, although it may cause some gastric irritation and burning in the mouth. It can also make your pets sick.

For the most part, Christmas trees are not toxic. However, cedar trees have caused an itchy skin rash. Pine, spruce, and fir tree are not toxic, but the needles can cause choking or obstruction when large quantities are eaten.

When purchasing a live tree, check for freshness. The tree should be green, with needles that are hard to pull from branches. Telltale brown tips and falling needles deliver a clear message: "Do not buy!" For better water absorption, cut about 2 inches from the bottom of the trunk and place the tree in water immediately. Be sure to keep the stand filled with water.

While there is a certain nostalgic romance about having a live tree, an artificial tree is a safer option. You can create your own tradition with a tree that is used year after year. If you do purchase an artificial tree, look for the label Fire-Resistant. If you choose a metallic tree, use only battery-operated lights. Whatever type of tree you use, place it in a wide, sturdy stand (rated for the size of the tree) away from traffic patterns in your house. Don't let it block doorways and exits, and be sure it is not close to any heat source.

Use lights and extension cords that carry the label of an independent testing laboratory such as UL (Underwriters Laboratories). If you reuse extension cords, examine them carefully and replace any frayed or damaged cords. For outdoor decorations, use only those lights labeled for outdoor use. Avoid decorating with easily shattered lights and ornaments and those with small parts. Be careful with icicles and tinsel, too. If the baby gets hold of either of these items, it's almost a foregone conclusion she'll put them in her mouth. Because they may block the airway or cause choking, and may contain lead and tin, it's a good idea not to use them on your tree until your child is old enough to know not to put them in her mouth.

Of course you want to buy toys that your child will enjoy longer than a day and a half, and you're likely to have a time beyond New Year's in mind. I don't want to put a damper on your enthusiasm, but keep this in mind: Improper use of toys can kill. They can strangle, choke, suffocate, poison, burn, and pierce. Remember the steps we took to make the nursery safe? Use those same guidelines when buying toys for all the children on your shopping list.

Toys That Can Strangle

For nursery safety we cautioned against strings, ribbons, and cords around the neck, across the crib, or anywhere near where the child is likely to be.

Toys That Can Choke

You've already learned the drill about small batteries, small balls, marbles, crayon pieces, keys, jewelry, paper clips, and buttons. If a gift comes in a plastic bag, make sure it is disposed of quickly—in a receptacle your child cannot get into. Remember: A toy labeled for children 3 years and older should be kept away from children under the age of 3 for safety's sake. This is not a matter of how smart your child is. Even if a toy has no warning label, inspect it for a possible choking hazard if your child is under 3. Check for small detachable parts and product accessories; security of eyes, nose, and mouth of stuffed toys; well-sewn seams of stuffed animals and cloth dolls. (Stuffing or pellets inside can pose a choking hazard.)

Toys That Can Suffocate

As your child grows, the list of toys that pose a suffocation risk grows, too. You've learned to remove soft toys from the crib. And you've chosen his toy box to make sure the lid won't slam down on his head or fingers and he cannot suffocate inside. Not allowing him to play with uninflated balloons and pieces of balloons is another step to avoid suffocation. More children have suffocated on uninflated balloons and pieces of balloons than on any other type of toy. This is an issue not just for small children; in fact, balloon-related deaths are more common among children ages 3 and older than among younger children. If you choose to use balloons, always supervise any play with an inflated balloon. Keep children from blowing up balloons, and immediately discard deflated and broken balloon pieces. Keep balloons away from children under 8 years of age. Choose Mylar balloons (shiny, metallic) over latex.

Toys That Can Poison

While balloons are not usually seen at Christmas or Chanukah, toys that can poison are in abundance. Batteries can be hazardous if bitten or swallowed. Remember our mantra: Everything goes in the mouth. The alkaline contents can leak from the battery and cause a chemical burn to the mouth, lips, and tongue. Swallowed batteries can obstruct the airway or throat. Miniature batteries may cause poisoning if swallowed, and they can cause internal burns if they become lodged in the esophagus or intestinal tract.

Some art supplies can contain hazardous or toxic substances. When buying art supplies for your children, including crayons and paints, look for this label: ASTM D-4236. It means the product has been reviewed by a toxicologist. If it is necessary, cautionary information will be included with this label. Do not allow children under age 12 to use art materials containing cautionary information.

Toys That Can Pierce or Burn

For children under 8 years old, avoid toys with sharp edges and points, electrical toys, and toys with heating elements. For children of all ages, avoid toys that include propelled objects. These can be turned into weapons. An added word of caution: Don't allow children to handle batteries or toys with loose or exposed wires.

Appropriate Toys

That's certainly a lot of caution to remember! You may be wondering, what can I buy? The National SAFE KIDS campaign offers guidelines for age-appropriate toys.

Infants Under Age 1

- activity quilts

- stuffed animals (without button noses or eyes)

- bath toys

- soft dolls

- baby swings

- cloth books

- squeaky toys

Ages 1-3

- books

- blocks

- fit-together and push-and-pull toys

- balls

- pounding and shape toys

Ages 3-5

- approved nontoxic art supplies

- books

- videos

- musical instruments

- outdoor toys such as a baseball tee, a slide, or a swing

Ages 5-9

- craft materials

- jump ropes

- puppets

- books

- electric trains (8 and older)

- sports equipment

A gift is not complete unless the proper protective gear is included. Gifts for older children, such as bicycles, skates, skateboards, or scooters, should be accompanied by helmets and other protective gear such as elbow, knee, and wrist pads. Remember when you used to open a lovely gift first, only to find batteries? Everyone laughed, but you knew there was a wonderful gift to follow. Perhaps a beautifully wrapped set of protective pads can act as a herald for a terrific new scooter. Prolong the enjoyment and promote safety at the same time.

Making a holiday safe is the first priority in making—and keeping—it happy. I wish you a happy, joyful holiday with lots of smiles in all the right places!

Review and Safety Checklist

✓ Before welcoming party guests, inspect your home for child hazards; do the crawl test.

✓ Take great care with open flames—including birthday, Christmas, and Chanukah candles; in jack-o-lanterns; with fireworks (even sparklers).

✓ When decorating for any occasion, avoid small objects and sharp or breakable items. Keep all decorations and flammable materials away from fire and heat sources.

✓ For refreshments for children under 6, do not serve hard, round food. Be aware of any guest's food allergies.

✓ Choose games that do not feature small or sharp objects.

✓ Choose gifts for children that are age-appropriate. Inspect all toys for small parts that may come off or out, posing a choking hazard.

✓ Promptly dispose of gift wrap, plastic bags, and ribbons. None of these should be used as toys.

✓ Avoid personal fireworks.

✓ On Halloween, accompany your children to every door if they go trick-or-treating and inspect the loot before allowing them to indulge. Better yet, have a party to provide a safe place for your children and their friends. Do not allow children to use cutting tools. Whatever the planned activity will be, ask others to join you in following the guidelines for safe costumes.

✓ Never leave electric holiday lights burning when you leave your home or when you go to bed.

Traveling with Baby

There's nothing quite like a parent's first outing with a baby. The exhilaration and feeling of freedom—away from the house at last!—is combined with the fear of various contingencies ranging from What if I forget her pacifier? to What if we crash? Between those extremes lie myriad possibilities.

Relax. By planning ahead, you can control most of those factors, including those you have not considered or imagined. Be prepared, stay calm, enjoy the trip!

Traveling by Car

All 50 states and the District of Columbia have child restraint laws. Laws vary widely from state to state, and many states are expanding their legislation to require booster seats for older children. More children in the United States are killed and injured in motor vehicle crashes than by any other cause. The proper use of child safety seats is one of the simplest and most effective methods available for protecting the lives of your young children in the event of a motor vehicle crash. In fact, it reduces the risk of death in passenger cars by about 70 percent for infants and by about 55 percent for toddlers ages 1 to 4 years. The correct use of a child restraint on every trip can prevent 70 percent of crash-related deaths and serious injuries to child passengers.

When should you purchase a child safety seat? Sooner than you may think! You'll need it when you bring your baby home from the hospital, so you'll want to buy the child safety seat (CSS) before she is born. Vow that day that you will correctly use an appropriate CSS every time you travel, even if you're going only one block to the neighborhood grocery. (Most car crashes happen close to home and at city street speeds.) Never hold the baby in your arms while riding in the car. That tiny infant, whose perfect little hand holds tightly to your finger, doesn't weigh much, but a crash can pull her out of your arms with a force of as much as 300 pounds.

Purchase a New Child Safety Seat for Your Baby

I highly recommend getting a new CSS if at all possible. The full history of a secondhand safety seat may be unknown. It may have been damaged in a previous crash; it may have been recalled; it may have been weakened by inappropriate use and storage. It may have missing parts or may not include a complete set of the manufacturer's instructions. Moreover, replacement parts and instructions may no longer be available for older safety seats, and the manufacturer may no longer be in business. Even if the seat seems to be in good condition, it may simply be too old. You should not use any CSS that has aged beyond the manufacturer's wear date or was manufactured more than 6 years ago.

The price of new car seats starts at about $50. Sometimes budgets are so tight that a used CSS seems to be the only option. If you can obtain a CSS only by accepting a used one, please take it only from a person you trust who can give you a full history of the seat. Do your research to be sure a) it has never been in a crash, b) it has not been recalled, c) it is not too old, d) a complete set of the manufacturer's instructions are available, and e) the manufacturer is still in business, so you can get replacement parts. You may not have to take second best, however; there are other avenues you may explore. Your state's SAFE KIDS coalition or the state highway patrol or health department may have a low-cost safety-seat program for families in need. Since the manufacturers of all child safety seats sold must certify that their products meet minimum safety standards set by the federal government, the best CSS is going to be the one that fits your child and your car. It must also be one that is easy for you to use properly, so that you will never be tempted to skip a step. For the CSS to be completely effective, it must be used on every trip.

Properly Match the Seat with Your Child and Your Car

Purchasing the most appropriate safety seat for your child and your car takes care. Go to a store with a wide variety of CSSs and ask the manager if he will let you install the store's display models in your car. Most stores are fairly receptive to the idea of bringing one model at a time to your vehicle. You may have to try several before you find one compatible with your car. If you choose a convertible seat, try it facing both ways before buying.

A newborn should always ride semireclined at no more than a 45° angle. This semireclined position will keep the baby's air passage open. As the child gains head control, make the seat more upright for greater safety. Sloping vehicle seats often need a tightly rolled towel or "pool noodle" placed at the vehicle seat crack to get the desired angle if the base of the CSS doesn't have its own adjustable "foot."

Age and weight determine whether the CSS should face backward or forward. Age, height, and weight limits on specific products may vary, so one must always read and follow instructions from both the manufacturer of the CSS and the vehicle manufacturer. The general guidelines are as follows:

From birth to at least 12 months old and at least 20 pounds, use an infant car seat or a convertible car seat in the rear-facing position. In this position, the safety seat cushions the infant's large head and entire back to reduce the risk of head and cervical spinal cord injuries during a crash or sudden stop. Never place a rear-facing CSS near an active passenger-side air bag. Newborns generally fit best in an infant-only seat. In addition, these seats are convenient to use because they are small and portable. Most safety experts agree that they are worth the investment. Look for one with an adjustable 5-point harness system. Be aware though, your baby may quickly outgrow the seat. Most infant-only seats will accommodate weights up to 20 to 22 pounds, but many babies outgrow infant-only seats because their heads are closer

DO IT YOURSELF!

Buckle your child correctly in his CSS

- Route the harness straps through the correct slots, according to the manufacturer's instructions.

- Tighten the CSS harness so the straps are snug and lie comfortably flat in a straight line on the child's body. If you pinch the harness fabric between your fingers and you can hold onto the tuck, the strap is too loose.

- Position the harness clip at armpit level.

- Do not wrap your child in a blanket, thick coat, or other bulky garment before strapping her into a restraint system. Instead, place blankets over the internal harness straps.

DO IT YOURSELF!

Do it right. Make it tight!

A common mistake made when installing a safety seat is the failure to get a tight fit. Here's how to do it right:

- Before installing any safety seat, read and carefully follow the safety seat manufacturer's directions, safety belt labels, and your vehicle owner's manual.

- Put your weight into the seat and lean forward while tightening the belt or LATCH straps.

- Test by grasping the seat at the belt path to assure that it moves no more than an inch to the sides or front of the vehicle.

than an inch to the top of the plastic shell.

When your baby's weight or the level of his head exceeds the seat's limits, be sure he rides in a CSS that is certified up to 30 pounds or more and continues to ride rear-facing until at least age 1—preferably longer. When you choose a convertible seat, whether for the baby's first ride or after he begins to outgrow an infant-only seat, be sure to choose one with a 5-point harness (no plastic shield) that can be adjusted without removing it from the car. Try installing it rear-facing and forward-facing to make sure it fits your car and is easy to adjust. The longer you keep your baby in a rear-facing position, the safer he'll be. The American Academy of Pediatrics recommends keeping children rear-facing to the highest weight or height allowed by the car safety seat's manufacturer.

From 1 to 4 years, 20 to 40 pounds or more, if your child can no longer fit into a rear-facing seat, put her in a forward-facing CSS with an internal harness. There are a few models with a harness that can be used up to 50 to 65 pounds.

From 4 to 8 years, 40 to 80 pounds or more, use a belt-positioning booster seat as a transition from the forward-facing CSS to the safety belt. Have your child continue using the booster seat until the lap and shoulder belts fit correctly. You can determine this easily using the five-step test developed by SafetyBeltSafe U.S.A.

1. Does the child sit all the way back against the auto seat?

2. Do the child's knees bend comfortably at the edge of the auto seat?

3. Does the belt cross the shoulder between the neck and arm?

4. Is the lap belt as low as possible, touching the thighs?

5. Can the child stay seated like this for the whole trip?

If you answered no to any of these questions, your child needs a booster seat to make both the shoulder belt and the lap belt fit right for the best crash protection. Your child will be more comfortable, too!

Know the Safest Place to Seat Your Child

As long as the child can be correctly restrained in the rear center position, it is generally considered the safest place for a child to sit in a car. However, the best rear seating position for your child really depends on wherever the seat fits most securely in your car and where you will be able to install it correctly each time. Statistics on fatal crashes indicate that the extent of injuries sustained in a crash is about the same for the right and left rear seats. From the center position, your child can't reach the windows or door latches, and he is insulated from all crash angles. No matter what age, every child should be buckled into a restraint system, and all children 12 and under should sit in the back. Since the most common type of crash is frontal, the rear seat is generally the safest place for children to ride, regardless of air bags. More than a third of one's protection is lost by moving to the front seat.

Not!

Never place a rear-facing CSS in the front seat of a vehicle that has an active passenger air bag.

Infant-only seats can be used facing the rear only, always in the back seat of the vehicle. Never place a rear-facing child safety seat in the front seat of a car that has an active passenger air bag. A rear-facing CSS located in the front would be very close to the dashboard, where the air bag is housed. The explosive force of an air bag is likely to strike the back of the baby's seat hard enough to cause a serious or fatal injury to the infant's head and brain. Nonetheless, adults should not fear using air bags for their own protection. Air bags have saved thousands of lives. Just make sure you are properly belted and have at least 10 inches between your breastbone and the steering wheel.

Side impact air bags vary greatly from model to model. Make sure to read the vehicle owner's manual to understand if you need worry about the interaction of child, safety seat, and side impact air bags.

Have Your Safety Seat Checked By a Certified Technician

According to the National SAFE KIDS Campaign, it is estimated that 4 out of 5 of CSSs are not installed and used correctly. To make sure you're doing it right, attend a free Buckle Up Car Seat Checkup sponsored by the National SAFE KIDS Campaign (www.safekids.org). Or visit the National Highway Traffic Safety Administration's website (www.nhtsa.dot.gov) to find local CSS Inspection Stations that provide safety checks year-round. A certified technician at one of these events will check your seat for proper function, installation, and recalls. He or she will then teach you how to correct errors or select a different type or model of safety seat, so you can be sure your child is protected on every ride. Some of the places where inspection stations are located are police stations, firehouses, and hospitals.

Register Your Seat

When you buy a new seat, be sure to fill out and send in the registration for it, so you will be notified automatically in the event of a recall. Manufacturers are required to fix the problem free of charge, usually by sending you a small part. There are websites that can keep you up to date on recalls. See Appendix D for more information regarding ways to learn about recalls.

Get the Right Extras and Install the Seat Correctly

Merely having the right restraint system is not enough. It must be installed correctly. Carefully read both the manual that comes with the safety seat and the instructions that come with your vehicle. Many vehicle safety belt systems, mostly those manufactured before 1996, require additional hardware to lock the belt in place, such as a locking clip that attaches to the belt, so always check your vehicle owner's manual. If you find that you do need a locking clip, you can usually find one attached to your CSS. You can also purchase a locking clip at a retail store that carries CSSs, or you can order it from the safety seat manufacturer.

As of September 1999, all new forward-facing CSSs must meet stricter head-protection requirements. To meet these requirements, most seats will have a top tether strap, an attachment that anchors the top of the seat to a vehicle. A top tether strap helps limit movement of a child's head in a forward crash, further reducing the risk of injury. Most pre-1999 vehicles don't have the anchoring system in place, but many after 1989 have predrilled holes. You may want to consider having your car retrofitted with this system. (Contact your local dealer or your manufacturer to see if a kit specific to your vehicle exists. Some dealers will install an anchor for free.)

All new child safety seats and vehicles—since September 2002—are required to come with a universal anchoring system called LATCH (lower anchors and tethers for children), which combines top tether anchors with lower anchors built into the rear of the vehicle seat. The LATCH system can make installation easier and more convenient for parents. Installing new child safety seats in new vehicles will no longer require the use of safety belts. But in order to use LATCH properly, the vehicle must have LATCH anchors, and the CSS must have LATCH attachments. If you don't have both anchors and attachments, use the vehicle safety belt system. A CSS properly installed with a safety belt is at least as safe as one properly installed with LATCH. (Be aware that most vehicles do not have lower anchors in center locations and almost no manufacturer will agree to have the inner bars used to allow for placement in the center.)

Make the Interior of Your Car Safer

First, when getting into the car with your child, enter the car away from the traffic side, and teach your child to do so, too. Check the temperature of the CSS surface and safety belt buckles before restraining your children in the car. Use a light-colored towel or blanket covering to shade the seat of your parked car. Before closing the door, check to see that no fingers are in the way. Look behind your car before getting into it and putting it into reverse. A child or animal standing behind the car may not be visible in your rear view window or side mirrors.

Now that everyone in the car is properly restrained—facing forward or backward, depending on age and weight—there are more steps you can take to make the inside of your car safer. Remove loose objects, such as boxes on the dashboard or in the back window. Even small objects can be sent flying in the event of a sudden stop or swerve, hitting you or your child. If there is a cigarette lighter in an ashtray in the back of the car, remove the lighter before a tiny hand picks it up.

Use the childproof locks if your vehicle has them. Otherwise, keep the doors of the car locked. This prevents your child from opening the door and falling out, and it prevents an intruder from opening the door when you slow down or stop your car. Locked doors also are less likely to spring open in the event of a crash.

For safety as well as security reasons, keep the car windows closed or opened only a few inches. In addition to this precaution, teach your child not to lean out or put any part of her body out the window.

When you leave the car, always lock it, even if you have parked in your own driveway. This will keep a child from getting in and becoming trapped inside, and it will deter an intruder from entering and waiting for you to return. Never leave your children or pets alone in a car, even for a minute. The temperature in the interior

DO IT YOURSELF!

Be prepared for emergencies in your car.

- Keep a fully supplied first aid kit on hand.
- Keep a flashlight with fresh batteries in your glove compartment, readily available.
- Carry a cellular phone in your car so that in case of an emergency, you will not have to leave the car. Preprogram emergency telephone numbers into the cell phone to enable you to call quickly.
- Be aware of your exact location at all times. If you need emergency assistance you should be able to give information about your location to a dispatcher.
- Always have on hand extra change, a bottle of motor oil, and a basic tool kit.
- Keep nonperishable snacks and bottled water on hand. In colder climates, keep blankets and a snow brush with an ice scraper in the car.
- Check your spare tire periodically to make sure it isn't flat. Carry a tire inflator, a device that can be plugged into your car's cigarette lighter to automatically pump air into your tire.
- Carry jumper cables and flares in your trunk.
- Register with a 24-hour automobile emergency service. Keep the card handy in your wallet.
- Always let someone know your exact route and anticipated arrival time.

of a car rises quickly, going to extreme levels that can kill. Don't think you've solved the problem by leaving the engine running so that the air conditioner can remain engaged. Your child can inadvertently move the car or get burned by the cigarette lighter. There is also the possibility that someone may enter the car and harm the child.

Be sure all children leave the vehicle when you reach your destination, particularly when loading and unloading. Don't overlook sleeping infants!

Make it a rule that children do not sit in the front seat or play with the steering wheel (or the car keys at any time). Children learn from the actions you model; when they have a chance on their own, they will try the front seat themselves.

Be a Safe Driver

Don't drive impaired. Obviously this means never to drink and drive, but it also refers to taking medication that may impair your judgment or reflexes. If you are taking any medication—including one purchased over the counter—check with your physician and read the product label and packaging about the drug's potential effects on your driving ability. Don't take a new medication and drive immediately afterward; find out the effect the medication has on your body. Don't multitask while driving; if you must talk on your cell phone while in the car, pull over to the side of the road and stop.

Obey traffic laws, drive defensively, and, on every ride, wear your safety belt properly. Never put the shoulder belt behind your back or under your arm or use a separate shoulder belt without fastening the lap belt as well. One day that precious baby of yours will be a teenage driver, out on his own. Teach by example.

Don't Let Your Child Ride Like Cargo

The cargo area of a station wagon or van is dangerous, and the back of a pickup truck is more so. In addition to the obvious hazard of being thrown from the truck—even a child under a truck canopy can be thrown out—there is the danger of carbon monoxide poisoning from exhaust fumes.

Keep Your Child Busy to Keep Yourself Calm

There are certainly times when you feel that, in lieu of having a pickup truck, you'd like to have an outside carrier for your children. You know the feeling? They're in the back seat, "touching" each other, crying, and whining "Are we almost there?" When they get on your nerves, you aren't able to concentrate on your driving (or on reading the map, if you're the navigator).

Keep them busy, especially if you're on a long trip, but remember the caution against flying missiles. Select soft toys, crayons, coloring books, other small paperback books, and games that won't be dangerous if there is a quick stop.

Traveling by Airplane

Statistically, flying is not as hazardous as driving. You are much more likely to be killed or seriously injured in a car crash than in an airplane. Nevertheless, you may feel less safe in a plane than in a car, partly because you feel less in control. If this is so for you, the best thing to do is take control! There are steps you can take to make the flight safer for yourself and your baby.

Fly Nonstop

It is more than inconvenient to have to change planes, running the risk of missing a connecting flight and racing through a busy airport carrying a baby or toddler and all her gear. A nonstop flight is actually safer. Most crashes occur during takeoff, climbing, descending, and landing than during the flight itself.

Sometimes changing planes cannot be avoided. Most airlines will provide assistance in transporting your child, CSS, and luggage. Arrange for this in advance.

Plan Ahead for the Appropriate CSS to Be Used on the Plane

All children 40 pounds and under should be in child safety seats on an airplane. (See sidebar below.) The same age and weight rules apply for planes as for cars. In order to sit facing forward safely, a child should be at least 12 months old and weigh at least 20 pounds. Rear-facing infant seats fit best on airplanes, but you can also use a rear-facing convertible seat. Children weighing more than 40 pounds should be secured by the standard-issue aircraft safety belt. Even though some booster seats and harness vests can be used safely in a car, they are banned from use in aircraft during taxi, take-off, and landing.

Although the FAA permits children under age 2 to fly in a parent's arms, imagine trying to hold on to a child in turbulence or in an emergency. Even if you are on a tight budget, don't try to save money by not buying a ticket for your precious child. Cut corners some other way, so that she can have her own seat, belted into an appropriate restraint system.

Inform the Airline That You Will Be Traveling with a Child

Don't keep it a secret. They'll let you on the plane with your baby—and grumpy passengers cannot vote her off!—but they may have special policies for transporting children. Be sure to ask. You may get a break in price, even though the child is, essentially, taking up as much space as an adult. Some airlines offer discounted tickets for children younger than 2 years who will be traveling in a CSS.

> ### DO IT YOURSELF!
>
> *Choose the right CSS for the flight.*
>
> Look for a label that says, This restraint is certified for use in motor vehicles and aircraft. Backless restraint systems (including booster seats) and harnesses cannot be used. A banned system will have a label stating, This restraint is not certified for use in aircraft.
>
> In order to fit on an airplane seat, the CSS cannot be wider than 16 inches. Any CSS can present some difficulty when installing with airplane safety belts, but if the label and size are right, it can be done!

If you can, avoid the busiest days and times for flying; this will make it more likely that you will have adequate space. If you select your own seat, be sure to choose adjacent seats for yourself and your child. (You may be on vacation, but it's no fair asking the flight attendant to babysit.)

The CSS must be installed in a window seat so other passengers are not prevented from getting out into the aisle. (That includes you, Mom and Dad!) And children cannot ride in emergency exit rows. These are additional reasons for informing the airline of the seating needs of your child.

Pack with Comfort, Convenience, and Entertainment in Mind

In your carry-on baggage, include food, diapers, medicine, and items that will keep your child entertained. Bring books to read to your child, soft toys, and coloring books. Avoid electronic games, which may interfere with an aircraft's navigational system during some phases of the flight.

The airline may provide special children's meals, so be sure to ask in advance. Sometimes a flight attendant can provide a deck of cards or a coloring book and crayons. You can accept whatever is offered, but don't count on it. Bring your own!

Become Familiar with the Aircraft

As you board the plane, take your seat and locate the exits closest to you. Count the number of rows to the nearest exits (toward both the front and the back of the plane). In a smoke-filled cabin, you'll be able to feel your way to the exit.

Check to see if there are seat-back telephones available.

Read the written safety instructions. You've glanced at them dozens of times, of course, but a quick review will prepare you to handle an emergency should it arise. And pay close attention to the flight attendant's preflight emergency briefing. Reviewing what you already know can help you act quickly if there is a need.

Keep Your Belt On

Throughout the flight, stay belted and keep your child in the child-restraint system. Come on! The belt is not that uncomfortable. You wear a belt for hours on a long car trip, and your child stays in her safety seat. Certainly being miles in the air is no time to be lax about using a safety belt. If the plane hits unexpected turbulence and the pilot must negotiate unusual maneuvers, you'll be ready; you won't have to decide whether to secure your own belt first or tend to your child's restraint. You're already prepared and protected.

Remember: Your Oxygen Mask Comes First

If emergency masks come down, grab the one dangling in front of you and put it on first. Only then do you grab the other oxygen mask and put it on your child. Don't even think about doing it the other way around. If your brain is starved of oxygen, you can pass out or get disoriented; in such a situation, you won't be able to help your child get out of the plane.

Don't panic! In the unlikely event that there is an emergency situation, you need to remain calm so that you can focus on the directions of the flight attendant and crew. Consider it role modeling for your child. If you aren't calm, fake it. Do your crying later, after you and your child are safe and sound.

Speaking of "safe and sound," you know that rarely does anyone fly from door to door. The appropriate safety restraint system will be needed en route to the airport and, again, en route to your destination. Find out ahead of time if the vehicle you'll be riding in when you leave the airport will have enough safe seating positions and belts. Uncle Ken means well, but your child will not be safe riding in someone's arms.

A Bike Outing

Any mode of transportation poses a risk of crashing, even something as basic as a bicycle. If you love biking, you may be particularly eager to have your child enjoy it with you. Don't be in too big a hurry to share the experience with your child. Never carry a child under the age of 1 on your bicycle, either in a bicycle seat, a child trailer, or any other carrier. Your baby does not have sufficient neck strength to support the weight of a helmet or to control head movement during a sudden stop.

A 1-year-old who can sit well when unsupported will have a neck strong enough to support a lightweight helmet; at that point he can be carried in a child trailer or a rear-mounted seat. For safety's sake, the helmet is an element that must not be omitted. Whether she is riding with you or riding her own conveyance—a tricycle or later, a small bicycle with training wheels—a helmet is a must. Start the child wearing a helmet with her first play vehicle, even if it is no more than a kiddie car that is powered by feet on the ground. Children who begin helmet use early are more likely to keep the habit in later years.

Choose a Helmet That Fits and Is Appropriate for Your Child

The helmet you use should be approved by the Consumer Product Safety Commission (CPSC) and be properly fitted. When worn correctly, a helmet can reduce the risk of head injury by 85 percent. A lightweight toddler helmet should always be worn by a young passenger to prevent or minimize head injury. It is, of necessity, lightweight, because a toddler's neck is not strong enough for a regular helmet. The correct toddler's helmet will come down low around the back of the head for more coverage. All bicycle helmets sold today must meet the CPSC standard. Look for a sticker inside the helmet. If the smallest toddler's helmet you can find is too big for your child, even if he is older than a year, wait until he grows big enough to fit into it. Consult your pediatrician for advice.

The sidebar tells you how to fit your child's helmet. Don't forget that your helmet should fit correctly, too. With the helmet on your head, look up; you should be able to see the bottom rim of the helmet. Look at your ears; they should be in the center of the V of the strap, which should fit comfortably, but snug. Open your mouth as wide as possible; if you can't feel the helmet hug your head, tighten those straps. Teach your child to do this exercise with you; have fun while learning.

If you let your child pick out the helmet, he will be more likely to wear it. Another way to maximize his helmet use is for him to see you always wearing yours. In addition to role modeling, you must keep yourself safe, so you can be there to care for your child.

Don't Reuse a Damaged Helmet

Bicycle helmets are designed for one fall. Any helmet that has been through a crash should be replaced, because even invisible cracks can greatly reduce its effectiveness in preventing injuries. Some manufacturers will replace helmets free of charge, so contact the manufacturer if your helmet has been involved in a crash.

DO IT YOURSELF!

Correct helmet fit is essential.

- Use foam pads inside the helmet so that it fits snugly, like a cap, and does not move on the head.

- Fit the helmet so the front is just above the top of the eyebrows.

- Adjust the two side straps so they meet in a V right under each ear.

- Adjust the chin strap snugly under the chin. Make it tight enough so the helmet pulls down when the child opens his mouth.

- Teach your child to wear the helmet correctly.

- Check often to make sure straps stay snug and the helmet stays level on the head.

Choose ASTM-Approved Seating for Bicycling with Your Child

The American Academy of Pediatrics recommends that children ride in child trailers pulled by the bike rather than carriers mounted on the bike. If you decide to purchase a carrier for the bike, I highly recommend that you have the seat installed at a bike store. Whether you purchase a trailer or a bike-mounted child seat, check to be sure it has a sticker saying it meets ASTM (American Society for Testing and Materials) safety standards. Although this is not a federally required standard, it lets you know the item meets specific safety criteria. Be sure the trailer or carrier has a rear reflector. Also look at the weight rating. Usually a bike-mounted seat can safely hold only 40 pounds or less. On the other hand, some trailers are designed to carry more than one child or loads up to 100 pounds.

Whichever choice you make, remember to purchase equipment from a reputable bicycle shop and to carefully read the instruction manual. Here are features your rear-mounted child seat should have:

- a high back

- a sturdy shoulder harness and lap belt that will fit snugly

- spoke guards that will prevent feet and hands from being caught in the wheels

A rear-mounted seat brings your child closer to you when cycling, but when you ride this way your bicycle's center of gravity shifts, making the bike less stable. After you have attached a child seat to your bicycle, making sure it is securely attached over the rear wheel, practice without your child. Get something like a bag of potatoes that approximates your child's weight and strap it in. Get used to the change in the way you balance as you ride. Only a skilled rider should carry a child on a bike. Keep in mind that if your child falls asleep in the seat, her weight is likely to shift, especially on turns. This will affect your steering.

Practice getting on and off the bike without swinging your leg over the child seat. This skill is very important if you have to dismount in an emergency situation. Never leave your bicycle unattended with your child in the child seat. If the bicycle falls over (which is likely if you aren't on it), your child will fall about 4 feet to the pavement.

A trailer offers a more stable and secure environment for your toddler. The extra space can also be valuable for bringing toys, drinks, snacks, extra clothing, and other supplies. When shopping for a bike trailer, be sure the trailer has a shoulder harness and lap belt to secure your child, mesh windows, and a swivel hinge to prevent the trailer from tipping over if the bicycle falls. In addition, the trailer should be designed with a roll bar that will protect your child in the unlikely event the trailer tips over. When pulling a trailer, stay in the trailer's width, from wheel to wheel. This is of particular importance if you are riding on a sidewalk and have to go around an obstacle, such as a light pole, or if there is a drop-off at the edge of the sidewalk or path. You don't want the trailer to go off the edge and tip into traffic. Because trailers are low to the ground, they are difficult for motorists to see, so a 6-foot orange or red flag for greater visibility is a must.

Regardless of whether you use a bicycle-mounted seat or pull a trailer, it is important to remember that you have extra weight on the bike, and it will take longer to stop and start. If you have gears on your bike and you don't know how to use them, this is the time to learn. Make sure the brakes on your bike are in good working order. Practice turns first without the child in tow. Turns have to be slower and wider. Always try to ride with another adult behind the trailer.

Avoid riding at dawn, dusk, or night. Be sure you and your child wear appropriate footwear, and do not wear clothes that can get caught in rotating parts. Wear bright, fluorescent clothing that makes you more visible in daylight, and attach reflective materials on the bike and trailer. Ride only in safe areas like parks, on smooth trails, and in quiet neighborhoods where there is little risk of encountering moving vehicles. Be extra careful near driveways and intersections. Avoid busy thoroughfares and bad weather, and ride with maximum caution and at a reduced speed. Obey all traffic laws. If the child screams a lot or is too fidgety, give up cycling with him for a while. Try again when he is older.

> **Togetherness on exercise equipment . . .**
>
> **Not!**
>
> You may enjoy bike outings with your child so much you're tempted to have her join you on your exercise equipment, especially on a rainy day when you can't go outside. Don't do it!
>
> Exercise equipment has weights that can fall and mechanisms that move and pinch. And she can fall off. (There is no safety seat on your equipment that should tell you something.) When the equipment is not in use, lock it away from exploring hands and feet.

Once your toddler is old enough to understand, let her know from time to time as you ride what safety measures you are taking. You will want to do this anytime you are out together, whether you are on the bicycle or walking or grocery shopping. Always keep in mind that your child will one day be doing this alone. Let her know how to look for cars, whether parked or moving, and show her how to modify her speed when others are walking or biking nearby. All this is a teaching-learning period. A toddler is not knowledgeable or wise enough to ride or walk alone away from home, but learning can take place long before that time comes.

After the ride is over, be sure the helmet is removed before your child goes off to play, especially on playground equipment. The helmet strap poses a strangulation hazard.

Not for Fun: The Shopping Cart

Shopping carts in the grocery store are for carrying items you wish to purchase. Coincidentally, the cart offers a place for your child to sit. You don't want a toddler underfoot at the grocery store, but the shopping cart is not a babysitter, and it is not a toy. There are certain rules of safety with this vehicle, just as there are with others.

Choose a Cart That Is Not Defective

The cart has a narrow wheel base in relation to its height, so the center of gravity is affected when you put a child in it. For this reason you do not want to set your child's infant carrier on top of it. The center of gravity would be affected even more, thus increasing the chances of tipping. Before you put your child in the seat, make sure the cart is not defective. You have probably, at some time, quickly chosen a cart and then, halfway down the aisle, discovered a rickety wheel. It's annoying to go clackety-clack all over the store, but annoying is not the word for it if your child is in the cart. If the cart is wobbly or unstable in any way, find another cart before putting your child at risk.

Strap Your Baby into the Seat Section of the Cart and Stay on Duty

If the store where you shop does not have safety belts, buy your own and bring it every time you shop with your child. At the store, buckle your child in snugly. Even after taking that precaution, do not leave your child in the cart alone. Stay right with it; don't walk away from it—not for a second. Don't allow another child to push it; don't allow an older child to hang onto the cart at the front or sides; and don't allow your child to stand up in the cart. Falls from shopping carts are one of the leading causes of head injuries to young children. Most injuries happen when a child has stood up in a cart or was climbing on it; a fall in the store means a cold, hard landing.

Review and Safety Checklist

✓ Before you purchase a child safety seat, match it with your car and by your child's size and age; make sure it is installed properly.

✓ Seat your child in the safest place in the car for him. Never place a rear-facing child safety seat in the front seat of a car that has an active passenger air bag. And never put any child in a cargo area.

✓ Remove potential flying missiles from inside the car.

✓ Be a safe driver and a good role model: don't drive while impaired and always wear your safety belt.

✓ Take along materials to keep your child busy and happy.

✓ Fly on a nonstop flight if possible.

✓ Let the airline know ahead of time that your child is flying with you.

✓ Pack a carry-on for comfort, convenience, and entertainment on the plane.

✓ When onboard, become familiar with the aircraft, keep your belt on, and if oxygen is needed, put your mask on first.

✓ For bicycling with your child, choose helmets that fit—one for you and one for your child. Both you and your child should always wear helmets while biking.

✓ Choose safe and appropriate bicycle seating for your child, either a child trailer or a rear-mounted seat.

✓ In stores, find a stable cart and buckle your baby into it. Don't use an infant seat on top of the cart's seat.

Appendices

A Room-by-Room Checklist

As was mentioned in the introduction to Part II, "Safety Measures for Every Living Space," you must learn to look at your home from your child's perspective, getting down on your hands and knees, crawling around each room. However, there is more to this concept: You must also consider whatever the child's perspective will be at the next stage. As soon as your child enters a new stage of development, begin preparing for the next, even when it means going out and buying new items. For example, you should have gates ready for installation before your child becomes mobile.

Once you get into the do-it-yourself mode, you'll begin to notice safety hazards outside your home. Anywhere you take your child—the homes of friends and relatives or day care—you'll want to carefully scan for anything that might cause harm. I don't recommend walking into someone's home and scooping up items as though you were a robotic hazard-crane, but there are polite ways to ask that certain dangerous items be removed. Certainly at your child's day care, the personnel should be glad for your input.

Any recalled equipment your child may use is a potential danger, and you should not be shy about looking for such items at the day care center, as well as at home. Inform your day care providers, family, and friends that they can obtain recall information on the new government website, www.recalls.gov, mentioned in Chapter 5. See Appendix D, "Recall Information," for ways to contact specific government agencies.

Do-It-Yourself Safety Throughout the House

Install It!

✓ Install smoke alarms on every level of your house and in every sleeping area. Change batteries once every year; test them monthly; replace the units every 10 years.

✓ Install a multipurpose fire extinguisher in the kitchen, where most fires occur. It's also a good idea to put a fire extinguisher in the basement and workshop. Learn how to use it before an emergency occurs.

✓ Install a carbon monoxide alarm in every sleeping area and place each one at least 15 feet from any fuel-burning appliance.

✓ Install ground fault circuit interrupters (GFCIs) if you do not already have them.

✓ Place safety covers over all electrical outlets.

✓ To keep large furniture from tipping, attach it to the wall with angle braces or anchors.

✓ Install window guards on all windows from the ground floor up. Each window designated as an emergency fire exit should be equipped with a quick-release mechanism. (Check first with your community fire department regarding local fire codes and window guard regulations.)

Lock It!

✓ Keep matches and cigarette lighters out of children's sight and reach.

✓ Keep children away from exercise equipment; store and lock it away after each use.

Test It!

✓ Make sure all fuel-burning appliances are properly vented and inspected annually.

✓ Test your home for lead-based paint if it was built before 1978. Ask your pediatrician or health department if your child should be tested for lead.

✓ Test your home for radon. (Call 800-557-2366 for more information.)

✓ Check your home to make sure no recalled products are being used.

Do It!

✓ Plan escape routes and conduct fire drills with the entire family.

✓ Dress children in flame-resistant pajamas.

✓ Enforce a no-smoking policy in your home.

✓ Eliminate sources of mold, dust, and insects such as cockroaches to help prevent asthma attacks. Keep pets and their bedding clean and off the furniture if possible.

✓ Repair or replace corded window coverings purchased before 2001.

✓ Use door stops and door holders to keep little fingers from being pinched.

✓ Prominently post emergency telephone numbers— including the poison hotline number (1-800-222-1222)— near every phone in the house.

✓ Enroll in an infant/child CPR and first aid course; every parent and caregiver should do so.

Not!

✓ Never leave your young child in or around water without close and constant supervision. These include bathtubs, toilets, liquid-filled buckets, coolers with melting ice, diaper pails, wading pools, swimming pools, hot tubs, fountains, wells, canals, ponds, lakes, or other bodies of water.

Do-It-Yourself Safety in the Kitchen

Install It!
✓ Install guards on stove knobs.

Lock It!
✓ Store household cleaning products, pet supplies, medicine, vitamins, alcohol, and other poisonous substances in their original containers, locked out of children's sight and reach.

✓ Keep your oven door locked.

✓ Use an appliance lock on the refrigerator, freezer, microwave, trash compacter, and oven.

✓ Plastic wraps and bags should be locked away if they are not tied in knots and discarded.

✓ Store knives and other sharp utensils in drawers or cabinets secured with child-resistant safety latches.

✓ For garbage cans a lock isn't necessary, but they should be kept securely covered and out of the reach of children.

Test It!
✓ Test the tap water in your home for lead, especially if you have an older home.

Do It!
✓ Use back burners and keep pot handles turned to the back of the stove.

✓ Use spill-resistant mugs for hot beverages.

✓ Keep your child in a crib, playpen, or high chair while anyone is cooking, away from the cooking area and away from any wall or counter from which he can push off.

✓ Make sure the floor is nonslip and free of grease. Promptly clean up any spills.

Not!
- ✓ Never leave your child unsupervised in the kitchen.

- ✓ Don't use tablecloths or place mats, thus avoiding the risk of your child's pulling a hot beverage or hot food down on herself.

- ✓ Don't set mugs of hot coffee and other hot foods near the edge of counters or tables.

- ✓ Do not hold or carry your child while holding hot foods or beverages.

- ✓ Do not let your child use the microwave.

- ✓ Never heat a bottle in the microwave.

- ✓ Don't serve round, hard food to any child under age 6.

- ✓ Never leave any liquid-filled bucket or container unattended.

Do-It-Yourself Safety in the Bathroom

Install It!
- ✓ Install antiscald devices in the shower and tub.

- ✓ Apply a rubber suction bath mat or nonskid appliqués to the tub and shower.

- ✓ Install grab bars in the bath and shower.

- ✓ Attach a securely fitting cushion over the tub spout.

Lock It!
- ✓ Keep all harmful items that are commonly kept in the bathroom—such as medicine, vitamins, cosmetics, grooming products, and sharp objects—locked and out of children's reach and sight.

- ✓ Place safety locks on all toilet lids.

Test It!

✓ Always regulate and test the water before you or your children get into the bathtub or shower.

Do It!

✓ Set the water thermostat to 120°F or lower.

✓ Use a rubber-backed rug on the floor for stepping out of the tub or shower.

✓ Always empty bath water immediately after use.

Not!

✓ Never leave children unattended in the bathroom, even for a few seconds.

✓ Never leave electrical appliances near water or within the reach of your child.

Do-It-Yourself Safety in the Nursery

Do It!

✓ Buy a new crib that meets current safety standards.

✓ Look for the JPMA label—the certification seal from the Juvenile Products Manufacturers Association—when you buy any baby equipment.

✓ Make sure the crib is sturdy, with no loose, broken, or missing hardware.

✓ Position any mobile or hanging crib toy out of your child's reach. Remove any hanging toys when the baby begins to push up on his hands and knees, or when he is 5 months old, whichever comes first.

✓ Avoid strings on infant products, including pacifiers and rattles.

✓ Make sure the crib sheet fits properly. If it is too loose or so tight it pops up from the corner, it can become a strangulation hazard.

✓ To reduce the risk of sudden infant death syndrome (SIDS) and suffocation, always put the baby to sleep on her back, on a firm, tight-fitting mattress. Remove all soft, fluffy, and loose bedding from the sleep area; this includes pillows, blankets, quilts, comforters, bumper pads, sheepskins, stuffed toys, and other soft products.

Not!

✓ Never hang anything on or above a crib with a string or ribbon longer than 7 inches.

✓ Do not place the crib or any other furniture near windows, blinds, drapery cords, electrical cords, or heat sources.

Do-It-Yourself Safety in the Living Room and Family Area

Lock It!

✓ Small objects, if not locked away, should be kept out of children's sight and reach.

Test It!

✓ Use a small-parts tester to make certain a toy is not a choking hazard.

Do It!

✓ Use safety gates at the top and bottom of stairs as long as an infant or toddler is in your home.

✓ Keep stairs well lit and clear of clutter; have light switches at both the bottom and the top of the stairway.

✓ Tack down loose carpet edges with carpet tape or tacks.

✓ Identify and remove poisonous house plants.

✓ Buy age-appropriate toys for your child.

✓ Push TVs and other entertainment equipment as far back as possible on furniture so they can't be pulled over by your child.

✓ Use corner and edge bumpers on furniture and fireplace hearths.

Not!

✓ Do not use scatter rugs. If it is necessary to have them, add a nonskid backing or nonskid mat underneath them.

✓ Do not keep furniture (including chairs, benches, tables, toy boxes, or bookcases) near windows or draperies.

Do-It-Yourself Safety in the Garage

Install It!

✓ Install an auto-reverse feature and an entrapment protection feature—such as a photoelectric sensor—to the automatic garage-door opener.

Lock It!

✓ Store and lock poisonous materials out of children's reach.

✓ Store flammable liquids like gasoline in safety-approved containers outside the home, in a well-ventilated, locked shed or detached garage, and away from any source of ignition.

✓ Keep all tools out of children's reach.

Do It!

✓ Empty any bucket right away after use, and store all buckets upside down.

Not!

✓ Never store flammable materials near a heat source.

Do-It-Yourself Safety in the Backyard

Install It!

✓ Apply cushioning under playground equipment—either rubber or synthetic mats or loose fill material such as sand, pea gravel, wood products, or loose rubber products at a depth of 12 inches.

✓ Place a cover over the sandbox when children are not using it, so that animals cannot use it as a litter box.

Lock It!

✓ Securely store lawn equipment and garden tools when they are not in use.

✓ After using the barbecue grill, properly lock it away, along with charcoal, propane, and the lighter or matches.

Do it!

✓ Enclose the backyard.

✓ Remove or fence in all toxic plants.

✓ Pull up mushrooms regularly, especially after rainy weather.

✓ Keep steps and paved areas clean and well maintained.

✓ Promptly clean up animal droppings.

✓ Keep your child indoors and supervised at all times when any outdoor power equipment is being used.

Not!

✓ Never take a child for a ride on a garden tractor or riding mower.

Do-It-Yourself Safety around Your Home Pool

Install It!

✓ Install a 4-sided fence at least 5 feet high, equipped with a self-closing, self-latching gate.

Lock It!

✓ Equip all doors leading to the pool with child-resistant locks that are self-closing.

✓ Store pool supplies and chemicals locked out of reach of children.

Test It!

✓ Inspect pool and equipment regularly.

Do It!

✓ When children are ready, enroll them in a learn-to-swim class or water safety class taught by qualified instructors.

✓ Make sure all children have constant adult supervision when swimming. No child is drownproof.

✓ Keep rescue equipment, emergency numbers, and a cordless phone poolside.

Common Poisonous Plants

D o not assume that if a particular plant does not appear on this list that it is safe. This is not an all-inclusive list. Call the Poison Hotline at 800-222-1222 to be sure.

Angels Trumpet (Datura species)
Autumn Crocus (Colchicum autumnale)
Azalea (Rhododendron species)
Black Locust (Robinia pseudoacacia)
Caladium (Caladium species)
Castor Bean (Ricinus communis)
Chokecherry (Prunus virginiana)
Climbing, or Deadly, Nightshade (Solanum dulcamara)
Daffodil (genus Narcissus)
Daphne (Daphne species)
Deadly Nightshade, or Belladonna (Atropa belladonna)
Delphinium (genus Delphinium)
Dumb Cane (genus Dieffenbachia)
Elephant Ear (Colocasia esculenta)
English Ivy (Hedera helix)
Foxglove (Digitalis purpurea)
Hyacinth (Hyacinthus orientalis)
Hydrangea (Hydrangea species)
Iris (genus Iris)
Jack-in-the-Pulpit (Arisaema triphyllum)
Jimsonweed (Datura stramonium)

Lantana (Lantana camara)
Larkspur (Delphinium species)
Lily of the Valley (Convallaria majalis)
Mayapple (Podophyllum peltatum)
Monkshood (Aconitum napellus)
Morning Glory (genus Ipomoea)
Mountain Laurel (Kalmia latifolia)
Oleander (Nerium oleander)
Philodendron (genus Philodendron)
Poison Hemlock (Conium maculatum)
Pokeweed (Phytolacca americana)
Privet (Ligustrum vulgare)
Rhododendron (genus Rhododendron)
Rosary Pea (Abrus precatorius)
Sweet Pea (Lathyrus odoratus)
Virginia Creeper (Parthenocissus quinquefolia)
Water Hemlock (genus Cicuta), most toxic U.S. plant
Wisteria (genus Wisteria)
Yew (genus Taxus)

Holiday Plants

American Mistletoe (Phoradendron flavescens)
European Mistletoe (Viscum album)
Holly (genus Ilex)
Jerusalem Cherry (Solanum pseudocapsicum)
Christmas Rose (Helleborus niger)

Vegetable Garden Plants

Potato sprouts (Solanum tuberosum)
Rhubarb leaves (Rheum species)
Tomato leaves (Lycopersicon lycopersicon)

Essential Safety Products and the Do-It-Yourself Shopper

When it comes to safety in your home, you must be the expert. This book empowers you to do that. Like any other expert, you need tools to enable you to do what must be done. This shopping list will allow you to check your supplies and quickly see what you need to purchase. These items can be purchased at hardware stores, baby equipment stores, and supermarkets and can be ordered from mail-order companies. Make sure all these items are properly and carefully installed and are well maintained. Please check them frequently. Remember, no child-safety device is completely childproof. Proper supervision is always required.

Tools for Food Safety

- Vegetable scrub brush

- Large-dial food thermometer for testing whole poultry and roasts during cooking

- Digital instant-read food thermometer for use near the end of the cooking time for beef patties

- Appliance thermometers for refrigerator and freezer (refrigerator, 40°F or below; freezer, 0°F)

Tools for Home Safety

- Doorknob covers

- Door locks

- Decals on glass doors

- Door stops and door holders to save precious fingers from being crushed

- Cordless phone for keeping a constant eye on your child

- Baby monitor (portable units suggested for carrying from room to room)

Tools for Fire Safety

- Smoke alarms for every level of the house and every sleeping area

- Flame-resistant sleepwear for your children (check the label)

- Multipurpose fire extinguishers for kitchen, basement, and workshop area

- Noncombustible escape ladder strong enough to support the heaviest person in the home

Tools for Emergencies

- Fully stocked first aid kit (see Chapter 14, "Preparing for Emergencies")

- Small bulletin boards or similar items for posting emergency numbers by each phone

- Fully stocked disaster supplies kit, including nonperishable foods, flashlights, batteries, and water

- Cell phone (to be used in the car, also)

An Ounce of Prevention

Tools for the Prevention of Choking, Suffocation, and Strangulation

- Small-parts tester

- Safety tassels, cord stops, and tie-down devices for corded window coverings

- Cord shorteners to eliminate excess electrical cords

Tools for the Prevention of Electrocution

- Ground fault circuit interrupters (GFCIs)

- Electrical outlet safety covers and outlet plates (Be sure outlet plug caps cannot easily be removed by a child and are not a choking hazard.)

- Power strip cover

- Cover for computer's surge protector

- Hair dryers with built-in shock protection

Tools for the Prevention of Burns

- Antiscald devices (used in conjunction with setting water heater at 120°F or below)

- Bath thermometer

- Guards on stove knobs

- Appliance lock for microwave

- Oven-door lock

- Spill-resistant mug for hot beverages

Tools for the Prevention of Poisoning

- Safety latches and locks for drawers and cabinets

- Child-resistant packaging for medicine and household products (remember they are not childproof)

- Carbon monoxide alarms for every sleeping area and at least 15 feet from fuel-burning appliances

- Appliance lock for refrigerator

Tools for the Prevention of Falls . . . And Cushions for Falls That Happen

- Window guards with quick-release mechanisms for fire exits; check local codes

- Safety gates for top and bottom of stairs (For the top of the stairs, use hardware that is mounted/screwed into the wall.)

- Power-failure nightlights for bedroom, hallways, stairs, and bathrooms

- Corner and edge bumpers for all sharp edges

- Nonskid backing on all rugs

- Rubber suction bath mat

- Grab bars for bath and shower

- Angle braces or anchors to secure furniture to the wall

- Cushioned spout cover for bathtub

- Auto-reverse feature on automatic garage-door opener

- Photoelectric sensor or edge sensor on automatic garage door opener

- Cushioning to place under playground equipment: sand, pea gravel, wood products, or loose rubber products for depth of 12 inches; or synthetic or rubber mats

Tools for the Prevention of Drowning

- Pool fence, 5 feet high surrounding all 4 sides and with self-closing, self-latching gates

- Toilet bowl safety lock

- Locked safety cover for spa

- U.S. Coast Guard-approved life preserver, life jackets, and ring buoy with line securely attached, or a long-handled hook to assist or retrieve a victim from the water

Tools for the Prevention of Harm from Firearms in the Home

- Gun locks

- Gun cabinets, vaults, or safes (one place for locking away unloaded firearms, another for locking away ammunition)

Tools for the Prevention of Harm Away from Home

- Reflective tape to be attached to child's outwear when she is out at dawn, dusk, or evening

- Bike helmet, properly fitted, meeting current national guidelines (See Chapter 16, "Traveling with Baby")

- Child safety seat that is correct for your child's age and size and for your particular car (See Chapter 16, "Traveling with Baby")

Recall Information

R ecalled products are those that have been found to be unsafe, hazardous, or defective. To provide better service in alerting consumers, the federal government has created one comprehensive recall site to which you may go for all types of recall information: www.recalls.gov. The website links visitors to the home pages of government regulatory agencies responsible for product recalls. You may still contact individual government agencies directly.

If you do not choose to visit the recall site on a regular basis, to stay current on this matter you may, instead, subscribe to the site's email notification of recalls. It is important that you, in addition, search through the government agencies' archived information for products you already own. If you discover that a product you own has been found defective, contact the manufacturer for further instructions. Contact the manufacturer, as well, for further instructions if you own a product that has been recalled. Report any unsafe product or a product-related injury to the appropriate governmental agency and to the product's manufacturer.

Do not neglect filling out and sending in the registration form that comes with any product, so the company can notify you in the event of a recall. You may also wish to contact individual government agencies for information about specific products. Here's how.

Consumer Products

Agency: CPSC—Consumer Product Safety Commission. This agency has jurisdiction over more than 15,000 kinds of consumer products used in and around the home and school and in sports and recreation.

Website: www.cpsc.gov

Hotline: 800-638-2772, staffed M-F 8:30 a.m.-5 p.m. EST

TTY*:   800-638-8270

                  *Telecommunications device for the deaf

Motor Vehicles and Related Equipment, Child Safety Seats and Tires

Agency: NHTSA—National Highway Traffic Safety Administration, U.S. Department of Transportation (DOT)

Website: www.nhtsa.dot.gov

Hotline: 888-DASH-2-DOT [327-4236], staffed M-F 8 a.m.-10 p.m. EST. TTY: 800-424-9153

Boats (Recreational Boats and Related Equipment)

Agency: USCG—U.S. Coast Guard

Website: www.uscgboating.org

Infoline: 800-368-5647, staffed M-F 8:30 a.m. to 5 p.m. EST

TTY: 800-689-0816

Food, Medicine and Cosmetics

Agency: FDA—Food and Drug Administration. This agency has jurisdiction over recalls involving the following: Food for human consumption, pet and farm animal feed, cosmetics, drugs and vaccines, medical devices, blood and plasma products, medical equipment, veterinary products, other biologics.

Website: www.fda.gov

Hotline: 888-INFO-FDA [463-6332], staffed M-F 8 a.m.-4:30 p.m. EST

TTY: none at present time

Meat and Poultry Products (Including Eggs)

Agency:	USDA—U.S. Department of Agriculture, Food Safety and Inspection Service (FSIS).
Website:	www.fsis.usda.gov
Meat and Poultry Hotline:	888-MPHOTLINE [674-6854], staffed M-F 10 a.m.-4 p.m. EST
TTY:	800-256-7072

Environmental Products (Pesticides, Rodenticides, Fungicides, Vehicle Emission Testing)

Agency:	EPA—Environmental Protection Agency
Website:	www.epa.gov
Telephone:	202-272-0167, staffed M-F 8 a.m.-6 p.m. EST
TTY:	202-272-0165

Helpful Resources

General Safety

American Academy of Pediatrics: *www.aap.org* or (847) 434-4000
Consumer Products Safety Commission: *www.cpsc.gov* or (800) 638-2772
National SAFE KIDS Campaign: *www.safekids.org* or (202) 662-0600
National Safety Council: *www.nsc.org* or (630) 285-1121

Specific Safety Concerns

Air Quality
Environmental Protection Agency—to learn about lead, carbon monoxide, and radon: *www.epa.gov* or (202) 272-0167. Also see sections in this appendix on lead, radon, and tobacco smoke.

EPA Indoor Air Quality Information Clearinghouse—to receive more information on reducing your risks from carbon monoxide and other combustion gases and particles: *www.epa.gov/iaq/* or (800) 438-4318

Allergies
American Academy of Allergy, Asthma & Immunology: *www.aaaai.org* or the patient information and physician referral line (800) 822-2762

Food Allergy and Anaphylaxis Network: www.foodallergy.org or (800) 929-4040

Arsenic Test Kits
Healthy Building Network: www.healthybuilding.net/arsenic/index.htm or (202) 898-1610 x220

Art Supplies
The Art & Creative Materials Institute, Inc.: www.acminet.org or (781) 293-4100

Bicycle Safety
Bicycle Helmet Safety Institute—to receive information on bicycle helmets: www.helmets.org or (703) 486-0100

League of American Bicyclists—to locate a class in your area that will teach how to ride a bicycle safely: www.bikeleague.org or (202) 822-1333

National SAFE Kids Campaign: www.safekids.org or (202) 662-0600

Breast Feeding
La Leche League International: www.lalecheleague.org or (800) LA-LECHE [525-3243]

Burn Prevention
American Burn Association: www.ameriburn.org or (312) 642-9260

Burn Prevention Foundation: www.burnprevention.org or (610) 481-9810

National Fire Protection Agency: www.nfpa.org, www.riskwatch.org, or www.firepreventionweek.org.

National SAFE Kids Campaign: www.safekids.org or (202) 662-0600

Child Care
Child Care Aware—to receive information about child care referral agencies in your area: www.childcareaware.org or (800) 424-2246

National Association for the Education of Young Children (NAEYC)—to search for NAEYC-accredited early childhood programs in your area: www.naeyc.org or (800) 424-2460

National Association for Family Child Care (NAFCC)—to get information regarding accredited family child care in your area: www.nafcc.org or (801) 269-9338

The National Resource Center for Health and Safety in Child Care—to check out the child care regulations and standards for any state: http://nrc.uchsc.edu/STATES/states.htm or (800) 598-KIDS [5437]

Child Passenger Safety
American Academy of Pediatrics: www.aap.org or (847) 434-4000

National Highway Traffic Safety Administration (NHTSA): www.nhtsa.dot.gov or (888) DASH-2-DOT [327-4236]

National SAFE KIDS Campaign: www.safekids.org or (202) 662-0600

SafetyBeltSafe USA: www.carseat.org or (800) 745-SAFE (7233)

Cribs
The Danny Foundation—a nonprofit organization devoted to crib safety: www.dannyfoundation.org or (800) 83-Danny [833-2669]

Emergency Preparedness
Federal Emergency Management Agency (FEMA)—part of the Department of Homeland Security's Emergency Preparedness and Response Directorate: www.fema.gov or www.ready.gov or (202) 566-1600

The National Oceanic and Atmospheric Administration/National Weather Service (NOAA): www.nws.noaa.gov

Fire Safety
National Fire Protection Agency: www.nfpa.org, www.riskwatch.org, or www.firepreventionweek.org.

U.S. Fire Administration: www.usfa.fema.gov or (301) 447-1000

Firearm Safety
Brady Center to Prevent Handgun Violence: www.cphv.org or (202) 289-7319

NRA Community Service Program (Eddie Eagle Gun Safety Program): www.nra.org or (800) 231-0752

Fireworks
National Council on Fireworks Safety, Inc.: www.fireworksafety.com or (202) 349-7127

Flying
Federal Aviation Administration—to receive information on proper use of child safety seats in aircraft: www.faa.gov or
(800) FAA-SURE [322-7873]

Food Safety
Environmental Protection Agency—to be advised about high concentrations of chemical contaminates in local fish and wildlife: www.epa.gov/ost/fish

Environmental Working Group—to get information on mercury in fish and on pesticides and other toxic chemicals in food and water: www.ewg.org or www.foodnews.org

FDA/Center for Food Safety & Applied Nutrition—to receive information on seafood products as well as general food safety: www.cfsan.fda.gov or (888) SAFEFOOD [723-3366]

Safe Tables Our Priority (S.T.O.P.)—a nonprofit organization working toward preventing food-borne illnesses and death: www.safetables.org; for information to assist food-borne illness victims: (800) 350-STOP [7867]

USDA/Food Safety and Inspection Service (FSIS)—to receive information on meat, poultry products and eggs: www.fsis.usda.gov or Meat and Poultry Hotline: (888) MPHOTLINE [674-6854.

Immunizations
Centers for Disease Control and Prevention: www.cdc.gov/nip or the National Immunization Hotline, (800) CDC-2522 [232-2522]

Internet Hoaxes
To check out whether email information you receive is a hoax: www.snopes.com; for health-related hoaxes and rumors: www.cdc.gov/hoax_rumors.htm

Juvenile Products
Juvenile Products Manufacturers Association: www.jpma.org or (856) 638-0420

Kids in Danger—a nonprofit organization devoted to notifying parents of dangerous recalled children's products): www.kidsindanger.org or (312) 595-0649

Lead Poisoning
Alliance for Healthy Homes—a nonprofit organization dedicated to preventing childhood lead poisoning: www.aeclp.org

Environmental Defense Fund—to receive a free copy of "What You Should Know About Lead in China Dishes," including a shopper's guide: www.environmentaldefense.org/documents/404_pubscatalog98.PDF or (800) 684-3322

National Lead Information Center: www.epa.gov/lead/nlic.htm or (800) 424-LEAD [5323]

National Lead Service Providers Listing System: www.leadlisting.org

Mosquitos/West Nile Virus
Centers For Disease Control and Prevention, Division of Vector-Borne Infectious Diseases: www.cdc.gov/ncidod/dvbid/westnile or Hotline (888) 246-2675

Personal Safety

Child Watch of North America—an organization that maintains a 24-hour toll-free hotline for information on missing children. To receive information on Kidsguard Safety Program and find out where you can get free photo ID cards and fingerprinting: www.childwatch.org or (888) CHILDWATCH [244-5392]

National Center for Missing and Exploited Children: www.missingkids.com or hotline for receiving information on missing and exploited children 24/7 (800) THE LOST [843-5678]

Pesticide Safety/Alternatives

Beyond Pesticides/National Coalition Against the Misuse of Pesticides—a nonprofit organization committed to pesticide safety and the adoption of alternative pest management strategies: www.beyondpesticides.org or (202) 543-5450

Children's Health Environmental Coalition (CHEC)—a nonprofit organization working to decrease children's chronic health and developmental problems linked with common toxic substances: www.checnet.org or (609) 252-1915

National Pesticide Information Center: http://npic.orst.edu or (800) 858-7378

Safe Pest Eliminators, A—to ask questions or order less toxic pest control products and live beneficial nematodes: www.unclealbertsantbait.com or (866) KILLANTS [545-5268]

Playground Safety

National Program for Playground Safety: www.playgroundsafety.org or (800) 554-7529

Poison

National Poison Control Hotline—to receive information about poisons in the home: (800) 222-1222
Washington Toxics Coalition—to receive information on alternatives to hazardous household chemicals: www.watoxics.org or (206) 632-1545

Postpartum Depression
Depression After Delivery—to receive information on causes, symptoms and treatment:
www.depressionafterdelivery.com or (800) 944-4773

Pregnancy
March of Dimes—to receive information about pregnancy, birth defects, genetics, drug use, and environmental hazards during pregnancy and other related topics: *www.modimes.org*

Radon
National Radon Hotline (operated by the National Safety Council)—to speak to a radon specialist or to order a low-cost test kit: (800) 55-RADON [557-2366]

Safety Training
American Red Cross—to learn about local chapters and which ones offer courses on CPR, water safety, and babysitting: *www.redcross.org*

Shaken Baby Syndrome
Child Help USA—to receive information, referrals and assistance in a crisis, staffed 24/7: *www.childhelpusa.org* or
(800) 4 ACHILD [422-4453]

National Center on Shaken Baby Syndrome: *www.dontshake.com* or (888) 273-0071

Sudden Infant Death Syndrome
First Candle/SIDS Alliance: *www.sidsalliance.org* or (800) 221-SIDS [7437]

Sun Safety
American Academy of Dermatology: *www.aad.org* or
(888) 462-DERM [3376]

EPA, SunWise Program: *www.epa.gov/sunwise* or Stratospheric Ozone Hotline (800) 296-1996

Sun Safety Alliance: *www.sunsafetyalliance.org* or (703) 837-4202

Tick-Borne Diseases
American Lyme Disease Foundation: www.aldf.com or
(914) 277-6970

Centers for Disease Control and Prevention, Division of Vector-Borne Infectious Diseases: www.cdc.gov/ncidod/dvbid/lyme/index.htm

Tobacco Smoke
The American Lung Association—to receive free educational material on smoking and lung disease and information on smoking cessation programs in your area:
www.lungusa.org or (800) LUNG USA [586-4872]

Travel Abroad
Centers for Disease Control and Prevention—to receive health information for international travelers: www.cdc.gov/travel or
(877) FYI-TRIP [394-8747]

U.S. Department of State, Bureau of Consular Affairs—to receive travel advisories about individual countries: www.travel.state.gov or (202) 647-5225

Water Quality (drinking water)
Environmental Protection Agency—to receive a list of state certification officers: http://www.epa.gov/safewater/certlab/labcint.html; to receive information about safe drinking water:
www.epa.gov/safewater or (800) 426-4791

International Bottled Water Association—the organization representing the bottled water industry: www.bottledwater.org or (703) 683-5213 or the information hotline (800) WATER-11 [928-3711]

NSF International—to receive information on evaluating filtering devices: www.nsf.org or (734) 769-8010 or
(800) NSF-MARK [673-6275]

Water Quality Association—to receive information about firms that produce and sell equipment and services and on evaluating filtering devices: www.wqa.org or (630) 505-0160

Window Safety

Automatic Specialties—for Guardian Angel Window Guards:
www.auspin.com or (800) 445-2370

Window Covering Safety Council—to receive information on window cord safety and free retrofit devices for repairing cord hazards on older window treatments: www.windowcoverings.org or (800) 506-4636

Storing Human Milk

by La Leche League International

The milk you express from your breasts for your baby is a precious fluid. It combines the best possible nutrition with antibodies, live cells, and other substances that protect babies from infection and help them grow and develop. When you make the effort to provide expressed milk for your baby for the times you can't be there for breastfeedings, you ensure that your baby continues to receive ideal nourishment and protection against allergies and disease.

You'll want to take good care of the milk you pump or hand-express. Think of it as a fresh, living substance—not just a food. How you store it will affect how well its nutritional and anti-infective qualities are preserved.

Human milk's anti-bacterial properties actually help it stay fresh longer. The live cells and antibodies in the milk that discourage the growth of bacteria in your baby's intestines also guard against bacterial growth when the milk is stored in a container.

The guidelines that follow apply to milk that will be given to full-term healthy babies.

Containers for Storage

You can use either hard-sided containers for storing milk or plastic bags. Hard-sided containers, either glass or plastic, do the best job of protecting the milk. Plastic milk storage bags, designed for freezing human milk, offer convenience and take up less room in the freezer.

The glass or plastic container should have a top that fits well. Containers should be washed in hot, soapy water, rinsed well, and allowed to air-dry before use. Don't fill them right up to the top—leave an inch of space to allow the milk to expand as it freezes.

Milk storage bags can be attached directly to a breast pump, so that mothers can collect and store milk in the same container. Some mothers use the disposable plastic nurser bags designed for bottlefeeding to store their milk. These are less durable and are not designed for longterm storage. They may burst or tear, but double-bagging can help prevent accidents. With either kind of bag, squeeze out the air at the top before sealing, and allow about an inch for the milk to expand when frozen. Stand the bags in another container on the refrigerator shelf or in the freezer.

Put only two to four ounces of milk in each container, the amount your baby is likely to take in a single feeding. This avoids waste. Small quantities are also easier to thaw. You can add fresh milk to a container of frozen milk as long as there is less fresh milk than frozen. Cool the fresh milk for 30 minutes in the refrigerator before pouring it on top of the frozen milk in the freezer.

Be sure to label every container of milk with the date it was expressed. If the milk will be given to your baby in a day care setting, also put your baby's name on the label.

How Long To Store Human Milk

Whenever possible, babies should get milk that has been refrigerated, not frozen. Some of the anti-infective properties are lost when the milk is frozen—though frozen milk still helps protect babies from disease and allergies and is much better for your baby than artificial formula.

How long you can store milk depends on the temperature. Follow the guidelines in this table.

Previously frozen milk that has been thawed can be kept in the refrigerator for up to 24 hours. Thawed milk should not be refrozen. It is not known whether human milk left in the bottle after a feeding can be safely kept until the next feeding or if it should be discarded, as is the case with infant formula. Recent studies have shown that human milk actually retards the growth of bacteria, so it may be safe to refrigerate unused milk for later use.

Where	Temperature	Time
At room temperature	66-72°F(19-22°C)	10 hours
In a refrigerator	32-39°F(0-4°C)	8 days
In a freezer compartment inside a refrigerator	Temperature varies	2 weeks
In a freezer compartment with a separate door	Temperature varies	3-4 months
In a separate deep freeze	0°F (-19°C)	6 months or longer

Expressed human milk can be kept in a common refrigerator at the workplace or at a day care center. Both the US Centers for Disease Control and the US Occupational Safety and Health Administration agree that human milk is not among the body fluids that require special handling or storage in a separate refrigerator.

To keep expressed milk cool when a refrigerator is not available, place it in an insulated container with an ice pack. It's a good idea to use ice and an insulated container when transporting milk home from the workplace or to the babysitter's, especially on warm days.

Using Stored Milk

- Human milk may separate into a milk layer and a cream layer when it is stored. This is normal. Shake it gently before giving it to the baby to redistribute the cream.

- Human milk should be thawed and heated with care. Just as freezing destroys some of the immune properties of the milk, high temperatures can also affect many of the beneficial properties of the milk.

- Frozen milk: Containers should be thawed under cool running water. Gradually increase the temperature of the water to heat the milk to feeding temperature. Or immerse the container in a pan of water that has been heated on the stove. Take the milk out and rewarm the water if necessary. The milk itself should not be heated directly on the stove.

- Refrigerated milk: Warm the milk under warm running water for several minutes. Or immerse the container in a pan of water that has been heated on the stove. Do not heat the milk directly on the stove.

- Do not use a microwave oven to heat human milk. If the milk gets too hot, many of its beneficial properties will be lost. In general, milk for babies should not be heated in the microwave. Because microwaves do not heat liquids evenly, there may be hot spots in the container of milk, and this can be dangerous for infants.

References

Arnold, Lois: Storage containers for human milk: an issue revisited. J Hum Lact 1995; 11(4): 325-28.

Barger, J. and Bull, P.: A comparison of the bacterial composition of breast milk stored at room temperature and stored in the refrigerator. Int J Childbirth Ed 1987; 2: 29-30.

Butte, N. et al: Human milk intake and growth in exclusively breast-fed infants. J Pediatr 1984; 104:187-95.

The Human Milk Banking Association of North America. Recommendations for Collection, Storage, and Handling of a Mother's Milk for Her Own Infant in the Hospital Setting. West Hartford, CT, USA, 1993.

Morbacher, N. and Stock, J.: The Breastfeeding Answer Book Second Edition. Schaumburg, IL La Leche League International. 1997.

Pardou, A. et al: Human milk banking: influence of storage processes and of bacterial contamination on some milk constituents. Biol Neonate 1994; 65:302-09.

Quan, R. et al: Effects of microwave radiation on anti-infective factors in human milk. Pediatrics 1992; 89:667-69.

Sigman, M. et al: Effects of microwaving human milk: changes in IgA content and bacterial count. J Am Diet Assoc 1989; 89:690-92.

Simonds, R. and Chanock, S.: Medical issues related to caring for human immunodeficiency virus-infected children in and out of the home. Pediatr Infec Dis J 1993; 12:845-52.

La Leche League International
1400 North Meacham Road o Schaumburg IL 60173-4840
847.519.7730 o fax 847.519.0035 o 1.800.LA.LECHE

For more information on breastfeeding check out our website: www.lalecheleague.org.

Index

About the Author

Photo by Wilco

Debra Smiley Holtzman is a nationally recognized child safety and health expert and a specialist on the subjects of injury prevention, toxic chemicals, food-borne diseases, and more. She has a law degree, an M.A. in occupational health and safety, and a B.A. in rhetoric and communication, and is the mother of two children.

Holtzman was chosen an "Everyday Hero" by *Reader's Digest* and was named a "Woman Making a Difference" by *Family Circle Magazine*. She is currently the Honorary Co-Chair of the Florida SAFE KIDS Coalition and was the child safety consultant for the nationally distributed video program *Safety Starts at Home: The Essential Childproofing Guide,* winner of the National Parenting Publications' Gold Award.

She is a favorite on regional and national television as well as on radio shows across the nation and has been featured on NBC's *The Today Show, The John Walsh Show,* and MSNBC. She has also been quoted in top print media, including *USA Weekend Magazine, The Washington Times, The Washington Post, The Boston Globe, Woman's World,* and *Parenting Magazine.* She is a contributing writer for *Today's Parent, epregnancy.com,* and *Ediets.com.*

Holtzman teaches infant and toddler safety classes at Memorial Regional Hospital in Hollywood, Florida. She is currently on The Discovery Health Channel as the safety expert for the popular weekly TV series *Make Room for Baby.*

SENTIENT PUBLICATIONS, LLC publishes books on cultural creativity, experimental education, transformative spirituality, holistic health, new science, ecology, and other topics, approached from an integral viewpoint. Our authors are intensely interested in exploring the nature of life from fresh perspectives, addressing life's great questions, and fostering the full expression of the human potential. Sentient Publications' books arise from the spirit of inquiry and the richness of the inherent dialogue between writer and reader.

We are very interested in hearing from our readers. To direct suggestions or comments to us, or to be added to our mailing list, please contact:

SENTIENT PUBLICATIONS, LLC
1113 Spruce Street
Boulder, CO 80302
303-443-2188
contact@sentientpublications.com
www.sentientpublications.com